ONE FOOT
in
EDEN

Also by J. Philip Newell
published by Paulist Press

Celtic Prayers from Iona

●

Listening for the Heartbeat of God

ONE FOOT
in
—— EDEN ——

A Celtic View of the
Stages of Life

J. Philip Newell

PAULIST PRESS
New York / Mahwah, N.J.

Published by arrangement with SPCK, London.

Cover design by Cindy Dunne

Library of Congress Cataloging-in-Publication Data

Newell, J. Philip.
One foot in Eden : a Celtic view of the
stages of life / Philip Newell.
p. cm.
ISBN 0-8091-3869-7 (alk. paper)
1. Spirituality–Celtic Church. 2. Life cycle, Human–
Religious aspects–Christianity. I. Title.
BR748.N495   1999
248–dc21   98-53159
CIP

Published by Paulist Press
997 Macarthur Boulevard
Mahwah, New Jersey 07430

www.paulistpress.com

Printed and bound in the
United States of America

To my three sisters,
Darlane, Heather and Japhia,
remembering our shared beginnings.

Acknowledgements

Bible quotations are from the New Revised Standard Version (NRSV) © 1989.

The publisher acknowledges with thanks permission to reproduce extracts from the following publications:

Edwin Muir, 'One Foot in Eden', 'The Original Place', 'The Journey Back', *Selected Poems*, © Faber and Faber, 1965.

Edwin Muir, *An Autobiography*, by permission of Gavin Muir, © Chatto & Windus, 1980.

T. S. Eliot, 'East Coker', 'The Dry Salvages', 'Burnt Norton', 'Little Gidding', 'A Song for Simeon', 'The Eagle Soars in the Summit of Heaven', *Collected Poems 1909–1962*, © Faber and Faber, 1963.

Anthony de Mello, *Wellsprings*, © Doubleday, 1986.

Kenneth White, 'The House of Insight', *The Bird Song*, © Mainstream, 1989.

R. S. Thomas, 'A. D.', *Counterpoint*, © Bloodaxe Books, 1990.

Contents

⸻⟶〰〰ᴿᴿ🄯ᴿᴿ〰〰⟵⸻

Preface

A book on life as gift, and especially a book about the different stages of life, is one that has inevitably released in me a great stream of memory. Recollections from every stage of life have welled up from the past. I have remembered all sorts of people who in all sorts of ways have been part of the journey thus far. My Scottish grandmother for one, Mary Ferguson, often has been present to me in my writing. She used to like to say with great vitality in her eyes, even well into her nineties, 'Ain't love grand!'.

At the heart of the Christian mystery is the conviction that the well-spring of life is love. It is from that source that the graces that arise in us flow. And so it is people like my grandmother, who have been love-bearers for me, that I would like to thank. They fundamentally are the ones who have shaped my sense of the essential goodness at the heart of life. They are the ones in whom I have experienced the truth that love looks deeper than wrong to reclaim the goodness of the image in which we have been made.

This book was initially written in much briefer form as a Lent study for the Anglican Diocese of Portsmouth. It grew in the first instance out of weekly meditations with a group of men and women of various ages and stages. It was then used by hundreds of small groups throughout the diocese as the basis for Lenten reflection on the graces of life. Many of the stories and insights in the book have come via these meditations and group discussions. I am grateful to those who have been part of this shared creativity. Most of all I would like to thank my bishop, Kenneth Stevenson, who in his large-hearted way has given me the space and encouragement to write.

Chapter 1 is especially dedicated to little Jerome from next door, who was carried in the womb and came to birth at the same time as this book.

J. PHILIP NEWELL

Introduction

The Scottish poet, Edwin Muir, in his poem 'One Foot in Eden', writes:

> Yet still from Eden springs the root
> As clean as on the starting day.[1]

Muir is pointing to a connection deep within us and within all life to the essential blessing of creation's first day. His words suggest that at the heart of who we are is a dimension of life that is rooted still in the original goodness represented by Eden. We may have lost sight of it. It may lie buried under other levels of what we have become, but it is there waiting to be rediscovered. It is the root from which goodness and creativity may spring up in us again.

It is this conviction that characterizes the Celtic tradition of spirituality at every stage in its development. In *Listening for the Heartbeat of God* I attempted to trace this primary mark of Celtic spirituality from its earliest manifestations in fourth-century Britain to the poetry and artwork of the Celtic tradition in the modern world.[2] The first teacher of note in the ancient Celtic Church, Pelagius, had taught that when we look into the face of a newborn child we are looking into the image of God. Similarly in the great poetic tradition of prayer in the Western Isles of Scotland, extending well into the nineteenth century, there was the belief that in the birth of a child the image of God is being freshly born among us. This was to speak not simply of what is true of a child but of what is most deeply true for all people and for all creation. God is the Life within all life.

This emphasis on life's essential goodness is not to pretend that there is no evil. It is not to deny that we and all creation are held in terrible bondages to wrong-doing and sin. As Muir writes, with reference to Jesus' parable of the field that was sown with good seed before an enemy planted weeds in it (Matthew 13.24f):

> And nothing now can separate
> The corn and tares compactly grown.[3]

In the fields of our lives, he says, 'evil and good stand thick around'. The deepest truth however is the goodness of the field and its corn. The weeds threaten to choke and stunt the good crop. Redemption in this model of spirituality is about freeing the original goodness that is in us from all that harms or inhibits it. The graces of God are planted deep within and need to be released from all that obscures or covers them. They are like treasure hidden in the fields of our lives.[4] The deeper we dig the more we will find of that 'treasure trove', as Muir calls it, wrapped though it may be in layers of accumulated darkness.

Christ is the liberator, the one who shows us the treasure that is within our lives and guides us in the way of its redemption. It is a goodness that is to be found again and again in life, in different ways and in the various dimensions of who we are. As T. S. Eliot writes:

There is only the fight to recover what has been lost
And found and lost again and again.[5]

Christ leads us not only to the treasure but through
painful encounters with the falseness of what is within
us as well. These shadows need to be comprehended if
we are to glimpse the treasure of God's life at the heart
of our lives. 'The gift half understood', says Eliot, 'is
Incarnation.'[6] The hidden treasure that Jesus points us
to is God's life interwoven among our life.

Birth then, whether that be our birth or the birth of
any living creature, is at heart a fresh inception of God's
life among us. Chapter 1, 'Birth and Holiness', explores
this theme of the essential sacredness of all that is born,
not only of our lives but the lives of those whom we
find it difficult to like or respect. It asks how we are to
recover our inner sight in order to see, as St John says,
'the light that enlightens every person coming into the
world'.[7] This is the light that is deeper than darkness
and has not been overcome by it. It is a holiness to be
reclaimed and respected at the heart of each life.

Chapter 2, 'Childhood and Innocence', looks in
particular at the grace that shines clearly in the eyes of
an infant. Has innocence been planted within us at the
beginning of our lives only to be left behind when we
move beyond childhood? It is a grace that bestows on
us something of the essence of God's life. How are we
to recover it and integrate its gifts of wonder and trust,
for example, into the experience of later life?

'Adolescence and Awakening', Chapter 3, considers
the huge range of awakenings that occur in our
teenage years when new longings and realizations
begin to stir within us. The percolating of so much
unfamiliar emotion and thought can cause tremendous

turbulence at certain points in adolescence as well, but at heart what is happening is a grace of awakening. The adolescent is experiencing a rising into consciousness of depths that have been hitherto unknown. What is it then that happens to this wave of awakening that can break upon us with such staggering force? Do we close ourselves off to it as an uncomfortable grace or open ourselves at deeper levels to discovering the limitless depths of God's image and creativity within us?

Chapter 4, 'Early Adulthood and Passion', explores the passion for life that comes to the fore in these years, whether it be in relationship or in the sharpened sense of injustice in the world. What is it of value in life that happens without passion? Conception, artistic creativity, and the determination to fight what is wrong and to work for the transformation of our world are all born of passion's fire. It is a flame that partakes of the passionate and wild creativity of God. In what areas of our lives does this risk-taking grace need to be rekindled?

'Middle Years and Commitment', Chapter 5, asks what it is that creates in us the desire to give ourselves to another and to family and the demands of wider responsibility. The grace of commitment is one that keeps alive the strength of our decision to love and care. Although love is sometimes covered over in us to the point of not being visible, it is at the heart of our life, made as we are in the image of the One who is Love. The inner assurance of that Love is one that frees us to begin to be true to ourselves and to one another.

Chapter 6, 'Old Age and Wisdom', looks at the grace that can arise out of a lifetime of experience and endurance. The grace of wisdom is one that finds expression in the letting go that happens when a tight controlling grip on life is relaxed. The old can bring a perspective that is characterized by greater detachment and stillness, in contrast to the engagement and busyness of earlier years. How, at the different stages of life, can we find patterns of stillness amidst the activity of our lives in which to grow in wisdom's way of seeing?

'Death As Return', Chapter 7, views death as the return of all that is visible into the invisible realm of God. It is the grace that can lead us home, to the end but also to the beginning and the heart of life. How do we open ourselves to the grace of dying, not only at our last breath but in every moment of life? How do we, as Jesus says, choose to die in order to more fully live? The way in which we let go of every day and every thing that is dear to us is related to the way in which we will let go of our lives. In dying we are offered the grace of returning or falling into what is deepest within us, the place of God.

The basis for this book is the Celtic belief that grace is not opposed to what is natural. Rather grace is given by God to liberate the goodness that has been planted at the heart of life. Grace is opposed to what is false in us but not to what is most deeply natural. The various chapters attempt to apply this understanding of the relationship between grace and nature to life's different stages. Grace then is given not to combat what we most essentially are as infants and adolescents, etc., but to release the innocence and passion and wisdom, for instance, that are rooted at the core of our lives, made as we are in the image of God.

While the book's starting point is from within the Celtic tradition, it draws for its method of meditation on another great tradition, namely the Benedictine. The sixth-century St Benedict developed a simple method of prayer in relation to Scripture known as *lectio divina*, in which Scripture is read and meditated upon. Benedict's method had been largely influenced by the fifth-century monk John Cassian, who interestingly had shown great sympathy for the Celtic teachings of Pelagius in his controversy with Augustine. The common ground between the Celtic tradition and Cassian's teaching is the belief that God speaks from deep within all that is human as opposed to over against it. There is a confidence instead of a suspicion around the practice of listening within ourselves for the truth of God, for deeper than any confusion or darkness in us is the light that enlightens every person.

What Cassian learned from the early monasticism of Egypt and then relayed to Western monasticism was a 'method of keeping our hearts still'.[8] The belief was that if our minds and hearts could be still and free from distraction we would hear intimations of the Word that was in the beginning and through whom all things have come into being. This was similar to the Celtic conviction, based on the mysticism of St John, that our lives and the life of creation are essentially utterances or expressions of God. This meant that in looking to hear the Word of God we are not to be looking away from life but rather to its heart. It meant in practice the expectation that God speaks not from some religious fringe but from deep within our lives and all life. Cassian's teaching that we could meditate in the midst of any activity,[9] for instance, bears striking similarity to the Celtic practice of prayer in the most ordinary contexts of day-to-day life.

The practice of *lectio divina* falls into three parts: *lectio* or reading, *meditatio* or meditation, and *oratio* or praying. In the early centuries of course *lectio* did not usually mean a literal reading of Scripture, for copies of the sacred texts were rare, as was the ability to read them. *Lectio* therefore in practice meant a rehearsing or reciting of Scripture passages from memory. One of the great attractions to Cassian of this simple method of meditation was its accessibility to both the literate and illiterate. 'Lack of culture', he said, 'is no bar to that purity of heart and soul which lies quite close by to everyone.'[10] The practice then was one of recalling Scripture and almost listening to it being spoken within ourselves, to the point of the sacred text becoming our own. The man reciting passages from Scripture, he wrote, utters them 'not as though they had been composed by the prophet but as if he himself had written them'.[11] They express his own deepest reality.

This is the method of meditation outlined in the appendix of this book and practised in the exercises at the end of each chapter. As we reflect on the different stages of life we can recall passages of Scripture and allow them to give voice to what is deepest and truest for us. As Cassian recorded from his conversation with the monk, Isaac:

> Our experience not only brings us to know them [i.e. the Scriptures] but actually anticipates what they convey. The meaning of the words comes through to us not just by way of commentaries but by what we ourselves have gone through ... We see very clearly, as in a mirror, what is being said to us and we have a deeper understanding of it. Instructed by our own experiences we are not

really learning through hearsay but have a feeling for these sentiments as things that we have already seen. They are not like things confided to our capacity for remembrance but, rather, we bring them to birth in the depths of our hearts as if they were feelings naturally there and part of our being. We enter into their meaning not because of what we read but because of what we have experienced earlier.[12]

The second part of the *lectio divina* tradition is *meditatio.* Having recalled or recited a passage of Scripture the practice is then to allow a single word or phrase from that passage to capture the attention of our heart. In the method employed in this book it will be a word or phrase that expresses some aspect of the stage of life that is being reflected on. The repetition of a phrase is designed to focus the attention of our spirit. It is one thing, as we all know, to find a quiet place and a quiet time for meditation. It is another thing entirely to find a quietness of mind within ourselves to be able to listen attentively within the silence. It has been said that our mind is like a tree with thousands of monkeys in it swinging continuously from branch to branch. Our mind can take us distractedly in all directions, forwards, backwards, sideways and somersaults, for no apparent reason. Having set aside a time to be still and know God, as the psalmist says,[13] we can be led fruitlessly astray by a busy and distracted mind. Cassian quotes his friend Germanus as saying:

> And so the mind is always on the move, and at the time of assembly it is pulled, like a drunk, in every direction and it performs no task competently.

When it is speaking aloud in prayer, it thinks of a psalm or something else. When it is singing it is preoccupied with something other than the text of the psalm. When it is engaged in reading aloud it remembers something it wishes to do or to have done. In this way it neither turns to nor leaves any theme in a disciplined or opportune manner. It seems to be a victim of chance. It has not the power either to hold on to or to linger over what pleases it.[14]

What Cassian teaches is a simple repetition of a Scripture phrase, silently repeated again and again in our hearts, as a way of being attentive to God at a level deeper than discursive thought. As the anonymous author of the great fourteenth-century English mystical treatise, *The Cloud of Unknowing*, later emphasized, meditation is not about our minds being filled with holy thoughts about God. Even good thoughts will keep us at a superficial level, and one that is prone to the distractions of other thoughts. Rather, meditation is about being filled with a sense of the presence of God, and of his love. It is with 'naked intention', as *The Cloud of Unknowing* says, naked even of thought, that we are to seek God in meditation.[15] This is not an anti-intellectual practice, but rather is to say that God is unknowable or beyond thought. He is deeper even than images. Although we cannot 'know' God, we can experience God and be renewed in the experience of our spirits.

The phrase that Cassian's teacher, Isaac, used again and again in meditation was, 'Come to my help, O God; Lord, hurry to my rescue.'[16] Interestingly these are the words that were adapted for use in the *Book of Common Prayer* service for Evensong, and have been repeated for centuries within the English tradition of prayer:

> O God, make speed to save us.
> O Lord, make haste to help us.

In the meditation exercises of this book a different phrase will be used for each chapter. This in part is because, as Cassian records, 'the sacred words stir memories within us'.[17] The repetition of these words from Scripture is intended to evoke memories of our experiences of God's graces at the different stages of life.

The third part of *lectio divina* is *oratio*, prayer uttered or spoken from the heart. *Oratio* is an expression of our heart's desires, both for ourselves and for others. There is no desire too great or too small to be expressed in prayer. A feature of the *lectio divina* tradition is the belief that our deepest desires are good. We know of course that there are other desires in us as well, which are destructive and confused. Do we know that deeper than those false cravings in us is the goodness of desire planted by God at the heart of our lives, yearnings for love and well-being, for creativity and new beginnings? The exercises at the end of each chapter will lead us towards an expression of our heart's desire.

All of the great traditions of contemplation and prayer in the Christian inheritance move us out in our spirits towards an engagement and passion for the life of the world. The *lectio divina* tradition is no exception. It is not designed to leave us in a type of self-contained vacuum of inner peace and awareness. In meditation we listen to the Word that is being uttered in the depths of our own lives in the conviction that the Word is being uttered also at the heart of all life. In prayer we do not step away from the world but move more deeply into the common ground that undergirds life. The hope of this book is that in becoming more aware of the graces of God hidden within the soil of our own lives we will be led to more passionately seek their rediscovery and redemption in the whole of life.

1 ✤ Birth and Holiness

'The child to be born of you will be holy'
(Luke 1.35)

What mother or father, holding a newborn in their arms, does not at some level feel that the child's life is holy? Similarly, which one of us after being creative, even in little ways in day-to-day life, in our kitchens or gardens or workplaces, does not feel often that the creativity from within us is a gift, something that has been born from depths beneath our understanding? The words of promise from St Luke's Gospel, spoken by the archangel Gabriel to the Virgin Mary, have been cherished as the words that announced the coming birth of Jesus. They have expressed also something of the hope that is in every person, for the Church has repeatedly wanted to say over the centuries that what is true of Jesus is true for each one of us. The term 'Son of Man', used by Jesus as a self-description even before the Church so proclaimed him, points to an understanding of Jesus as the One whose life speaks of what is true for all people. At the birth of every child, and at the birth of every good creativity in our lives, can be spoken the words, 'This is holy for its life is of God.' The birth or creativity is to be reverenced because its source is something immeasurably deeper than ourselves, even though it issues from within us.

What does this mean for us and for how we view and treat ourselves? What does it mean in relation to the children born of us, to our parenting of them as essentially sons and daughters of God? What does it mean for our relationships with all people and with the whole of creation, as at heart sacred? Yes, of course there is much in us that is not holy, but the gospel promise is that at our birth we bear deep within ourselves the sacredness of God's image. As St John the Evangelist says in the prologue to his Gospel, this is 'the true light that enlightens every person coming into the world'.[1] This is the Light within all light, the Life at the heart of all that has life. So clearly did the early British Church see this that Pelagius and those who came after him in the Celtic tradition wanted to say that when we look into the face of a newborn baby we are looking into the image of God. The life of God is born anew among us in the birth of a child. Similarly the ninth-century Irish theologian, John Scotus Eriugena, said that if we were to extract all goodness from creation everything and all people would cease to exist, for at the core of all life is the goodness of God. It is God's Life that sustains all life, and it is God's Soul that indwells every living soul.

The vision expressed in the book of Hebrews is that all that is visible has come forth from what is invisible, all that is seen has had its origin in what cannot be seen.[2] It is pointing to a Ground of Being that is spiritual and from which all that is material has had its inception. This is diametrically opposed to what is most popularly held to be true in the Western world. Is life not simply born from what is physical, one form of

13

matter giving rise to another material life-form in the great stream of evolution? St Augustine of Hippo, one of the greatest Christian teachers of the early centuries, spoke of the need to restore to health the eye of the heart whereby God may be seen. This is a way of seeing that looks deeper than the physical.

There are of course different ways of seeing, and, as we all know, some are more faithful to reality than others. There is the story of the woman, for example, who thought she recognized a man from her past. 'You used to be so tall and now you are quite short,' she said, 'and you used to be dark haired but now you are fair.' The man responded, 'I think you must be confusing me with someone else. My name is MacIntosh'; to which the woman replied, 'So you have even changed your name!'

We sometimes see merely what we want to see rather than what is most truly there. Our materialistic age is one that tends to look exclusively to the physical. And it has preferred to deny in its outlook on life what we all at some level know to be true, all that is physical is passing. To place ultimate confidence in the outward alone is to build on impermanent foundations. This is not to disparage the physical, for the world of creation, including the human body, has a sacramental quality. Within the created the light of the Uncreated can be glimpsed. As Pelagius said, 'Narrow shafts of divine light pierce the veil that separates heaven from earth.'[3] The matter of the universe is shot through with spirit. The root of creation's outward glory however is deeper than its physicalness. We need a healing of the inner eye if we are to glimpse the Life that is born within all life. Thus will we come to see the holiness at the heart of each child and of all creativity.

A recovery of our inner sight will free us to see not only from without but from within. At the heart of life is the eternal womb, as Job says, from which the waters of life have burst forth.[4] From that source comes 'the soul of every living thing and the breath of every human being'.[5] We know what it is to see a young shoot pushing its way up out of the soil and drawing sustenance from the earth. Do we also see with inner sight that each plant, each creature, each human being is born at heart from holy soil? This is to see life from within the dark and unknowable place of God, looking as it were from the womb of life onto all that has been born into creation. This we can do in reflecting on the beginnings of all things, whether that be the formation of minute life-forms on earth or the creation of the magnificent stars of distant galaxies. The Womb at the heart of life is holy. All that has been born into creation bears within itself something of God's holiness.

To speak of the 'darkness' of the place from which all things have come is to point to the unknowable depths of the Mystery. It is not however to suggest a fallenness at the heart of creation. Dualistic thinking has tended to tear the spiritual away from the material. As a result spirit has been viewed as 'light' and matter as 'dark'. Implied in this is the belief that the matter of creation, including the matter of our bodies, is essentially godless. Similarly the preconception in much Western Christian teaching has been that the sexual act accompanying procreation is essentially a physical and lustful act. The conclusion has been that all that is born is sinful at its core and remains so until the grace of baptism plants a

15

goodness in the soul. Such a regenerated goodness in the soul however still tends to be viewed as foreign to the body.

It was particularly the Celtic branch of Christianity in the West that opposed this view. The early British Church was not prepared to say that a newborn child was at heart sinful. Its conviction was rather that of the Genesis account, accentuating the goodness of all that has been created.[6] Similarly it shared the vision of St John who in the prologue to his Gospel writes of all things as having come into being through the Word.[7] We, including our bodies and the whole of creation, are seen in essence as utterances of God. We have been spoken into being by the Word that was in the beginning. The Celtic Church expressed this artistically in its recurring patterns of interwoven strands in manuscript illumination and stonework. This represented the inseparable interweaving of the spiritual and the material, of heaven and earth. The matter of all that is born is seen as penetrated with spirit, and as enlivened by it. This is not to say that matter is confused with spirit. The former comes and goes. It is born and dies, but at heart matter has been expressed into being by spirit.

R. S. Thomas, the Welsh poet, in his work 'A. D.', writes of a confused way of seeing in which the beginnings of life are viewed as 'a dark past'.[8] If we hold the lens aright, he says, we will see a dawn that had about it 'the brightness of flowers'. Like Muir's roots to Eden that connect us still with the goodness of the first day, Thomas writes of discovering our 'incipient wings' rather than 'the slime' from which we think we have emerged. The Celtic poet, Yeats, similarly writes of 'the holy tree' at the heart of life, from which beauty and goodness spring. This way of seeing is threatened, he

says, by 'the bitter glass' held up before our eyes by
demons.[9] If we gaze through that glass our eyes 'grow
all unkind' and we see only 'a fatal image' within ourselves. To see the holy tree within, on the other hand,
is to be freed to see life at its heart as good.

An old woman recollected from her childhood the
experience of seeing her stillborn sister laid out on a
bed. While she had been aware of her mother's pain,
her memory was primarily that of the still beauty of
the child. She spoke of the experience as having shaped
her sense of the holiness of newborn life as well as
her understanding of life as journey from God and to
God. That particular little life, of the briefest duration,
conveyed to her an impression of the Life from which
all life comes.

What is it that the birth of a child, and even the birth
of a stillborn child, can bring? The newborn carries
within herself intimations of the One from whom she
has come. As Wordsworth writes in 'Intimations of
Immortality':

> Not in entire forgetfulness,
> And not in utter nakedness,
> But trailing clouds of glory do we come
> From God, who is our home.[10]

The 'clouds of glory' that a child trails into the world
speak of God as life's beginning and life's home. The
message, even though received for the most part at
depths beneath our consciousness, is of the holiness
of all life, though often it will be a holiness that lies
hidden.

It is not of course just at the *birth* of our children that
we have a sense of gift from God. It can also be when
we first learn of their conception and begin to wait

with expectation for their arrival. The conception of Christ as related in St Luke's Gospel is accompanied by angelic appearance, which in the Bible signifies the presence of the Holy and intimates the coming of a great event. Rather than conception being seen purely in terms of a physical act, it is an inception of God's life among us. Within conception a deeper mystery is taking place in which life is issuing from the invisible realm of God into the visible world of creation. At the planting of seeds in the field, at the germinating of new life in the animal world, and at the conception of each child, a gift from God is being conceived. Similarly, when goodness and truth, or when beauty of spirit and love are conceived within us or among us, in our minds and hearts and relationships, let us know that God is sowing in the ground of our lives something that is sacred and to be cherished.

When a mother first feels the child within her move and kick there is the excitement of knowing that she carries within herself another life. And similarly there can be delight in a father listening for the early stirrings of life in his wife's womb. Such a man and woman will sense at the deepest of levels that a promise from God is being fulfilled somehow in their lives and that while the life of the child has come from them, it has come also from beyond them.

Given the wonder of what is transpiring in conception and the development of a child in the womb, is it not terrible when an expectant mother is discouraged, either by the fashions of her culture or by the limited perspective of her partner, from seeing the physical beauty of her pregnancy? Is there a shape that speaks more emphatically of the fecundity of life and the mystery of God born in and among us? Instead of a woman ever feeling ashamed of her pregnant figure she is rather to know its beauty, like the heavily laden fruitfulness of an autumn tree. She can be like an icon for us, a sign of the wonderful mystery that is true of all life, for we all carry within us something of the otherness of God, closer to us than our very breath.

Carrying a child can of course have a great discomfort about it, just as being true to the life of God within us is often a struggle. Listening to what God is raising into consciousness will bring with it sometimes all sorts of discomfort and disturbance. The same can be said about the pain of actually giving birth, or the pain of delivering the creativities that have been stirring within us. The primal scream which sounds from the depths of a woman just before delivery carries within it something of the pain of birth pangs that have been known in people and in creation since the beginning of time. The way in which birth can tear a body is true of great creativities in other realms of life as well. We need only think, for instance, of the pain of freedom's birth in a place such as South Africa, or the way in which forgiveness or truth being born among us and in our relationships will sometimes be with terrible agony. Even in the strongest of relationships love is fully born only in and through the pain of struggle and personal sacrifice. Similarly fresh discoveries in the sciences, or artistic creativities and new ways of seeing and understanding in cultures will come usually only through what is like the sweat and tears of labour.

Mixed with the pain of giving birth is of course the sheer joy that comes with first holding a newborn, looking into the child's face and knowing that a gift from God has been born. And have we not all experienced some of the celebration that follows births and

19

creative moments? The retelling of St Luke's birth narrative, with its sky full of light and songs of glory, celebrates the holiness of the Child that was born, and points to the holiness of every child and of every good creativity. For at its deepest level the story is expressing the beauty and the goodness that can be painfully delivered from within our lives, and the hope of what is yet to be born. As Anthony de Mello, the Indian Jesuit priest, said, 'Listen to the song the angels sang the day you were born.'[11] Listen to the song that is being sung whenever creativity comes to birth.

If we recover this way of seeing, will we not begin to glimpse something of the profusion of holiness that is being born each instant in the earth and sea and skies around us? And in our cities will we not be led to see our post-natal wards anew as cradles of hope in which the image of God is being freshly born among us, not only in our cherished and healthy children but in the so-called 'unwanted' and neglected? To discern the holy in all that has been born may at times seem impossible, and especially in those whom we do not like or in those who have committed terrible crimes or in ourselves when we have been untrue. But central to the gospel is the conviction that the goodness of God is there at the heart of each life yearning to be set free, to be born again. The mystery of which we are a part, says St Paul, is that the whole of creation is groaning in labour for the fullness of what God is desiring to give birth to in our lives and in all life.[12]

Exercise

Sitting comfortably but alert, with your back upright, begin to repeat silently the phrase, 'The child to be born of you will be holy.' When distractions occur, as they invariably will, simply return to the phrase as a way of focussing the attention of your spirit.

Allow the repetition of the phrase to be spoken in time with your breathing. Try, for instance, to repeat silently the words as you breathe down. 'The child to be born of you will be holy.' Let the phrase be sown within you. Allow it to rest in your depths. Then as you breathe up be conscious that what is born from God's depths of life in you is holy.

It is not so much a matter of speaking the words as listening to them being uttered within you. These are words of promise spoken to you and to what is true at the heart of all life. Listen to them in silence for fifteen minutes. Know that the words are spoken from the depths of who you are, where God dwells. Allow them to evoke memories and images, not at this stage to actively think about, but simply to receive and be aware of.

At the end of the fifteen minutes of meditation move from the simple repetition of words to an expression of your heart's desire. Silently utter within yourself a prayer of what it is you desire most deeply in your own life and in the life of the world. Finish your prayer by saying the Lord's Prayer.

2 ✤ Childhood and Innocence

‘To such as these belongs the kingdom of God’
(Luke 18.16)

What are our memories of early childhood? And what images come to mind when we think back to the infancy of our children and of little ones we have known? It is likely that we will remember a mixture of happy and sad times, and that our images will be both of children laughing and crying, of skipping as well as screaming. We will remember early childhood's immediacy of dream life and the realm of the imaginary while probably recollecting also its vividness of nightmares and fears. What is it that Jesus is pointing to in a little child when he says, 'To such as these belongs the kingdom of God'? What is it in our children and in all children, and what was it in our own infancy and in the infancy of all people that is being referred to here? God has given us at our birth something that is of the essence of his life. It is at the beginning of who we have been created to be and it is at the end or heart of our journey as something that we are called to rediscover.

In the innocence of a child we see most clearly the beauty of the image in which we have been made.

There is the beautiful countenance of a sleeping child, irresistible to gaze at, or the awakened delight in an infant's eyes at some new discovery. In *Songs of Innocence* the poet William Blake says:

> Sweet babe, in thy face
> Holy image I can trace.[1]

What is it then that happens to this innocence in us? Often it is spoken of as something that will inevitably be 'lost', meaning that experience is sure to erase it. We see it shining in the eyes of our newborn, and then relatively early on we observe it beginning to be threatened until finally a harsh experience or a breaking of trust starts to obscure what once shone so purely in the child. But is it right to say that the grace of innocence has been lost at such a moment? Is it not truer to say that it has been covered over by the streaks of experience's darkness and that it needs to be recovered again and again in new ways at the different stages of life? Did God plant innocence deep within us in our mothers' wombs for it simply to be left behind when we moved beyond early childhood?

In another collection of poems, *Songs of Experience*, Blake explores what it is that happens to this 'holy image' that shines so clearly in childhood's innocence. In 'Little Girl Lost', he writes:

> Lost in desart wild
> Is your little child.[2]

The lines speak of the confusions and dangers into which we enter with experience, the wrong turnings taken within ourselves and in relationship as well as those imposed upon us from without. There is the impression of an interminable maze, a dark jungle of social and psychological experiences, out of which the innocent child will never be seen again. In 'The Little Girl Found', Blake describes the fear that consumes the child's mother and father, who imagine that their little girl, Lyca, has either been starved to death or torn to pieces by vicious beasts. In the desert however they meet a lion, great and crowned, whose words to them are:

> 'Follow me,' he said;
> 'Weep not for the maid;
> In my palace deep
> Lyca lies asleep.'[3]

Asleep then, not dead, is the child of innocence, apparently lost forever, but in fact protected in an inviolable shelter waiting to be found.

Lost but alive is very different of course from being lost and dead. If our 'lost' innocence is viewed in the latter way we will live as people who are cut off from what has been most deeply planted within us. We will be in danger of living out of a false conception that the 'holy image' in us has been erased. We will not believe that there is in us a true core of our life's innocent beginnings from which we may still draw. Related to this will be the tendency to consider the ways in which a child sees and interprets reality as being of little value. The realm of myth and fable and imagination will be dismissed as mere fantasy.

Blake's sense of the innocent child in us, lost yet alive, is an important part of his vision. Even more important, in terms of the rediscovery of the child, is his pointing to the One who holds and protects that part of us from being utterly destroyed. No matter what has happened outwardly, whether through neglect or abuse, our inner 'holy image' is being held in a safety that cannot be violated, and it is waiting to be redis-covered. The inviolable nature of that 'palace' or sanc-tuary is not of our own doing. Rather it is a gift. 'On his head a crown', the poem's description of the great lion who both protects the child and leads the way to her rediscovery, is Blake's way of pointing to the grace of Christ's presence and of being guided to find the holy image in us that has been covered over. It is not simply a matter of knowing our need, although without that realization our search cannot begin. It is a matter of being open to the grace of guidance from the One who has sheltered our child and knows where she is to be found.

The disciples in St Luke's story try to divert Jesus' attention from the longings of parents in relation to their children. In terms of what is important to the disciples, the innocence of a child and a blessing of that innocence does not rank high. Maybe this is true for most of us much of the time as well, but for nearly all of us at least some of the time there is another truth. We need only walk along a city street with a little child in a pushchair to know how eager people are to look into the face of a baby. Even men and women whom we might have expected to be too hardened or too busy will surprise us by smiling at a child. I remember entering an almost deserted and very sleepy village square in a Greek town on the island of Patmos. If I had not been walking with my two-year-old daughter it would have remained a sleepy place with the expres-sionless faces of a few old men dozing in the shadows. But when they saw an innocent little face blinking at them through the bright sunlight of midday, they came to life, and one of them shuffled off to emerge a moment later with handfuls of fruit and sweets.

Similarly what do we make of the almost universal indignation that rages in people when the safety and trust of a child is threatened or violated? These things speak of a type of resonance with the innocence of childhood. Something of the child is still deep within us. It may be covered over by the wrongs and pains that we have witnessed or been part of in life, but it is still there. Jesus' words to the disciples point to the kingdom of God belonging to that part of us.

It is important to recognize that the innocence of a child is not always beautifully apparelled. This is true whether we are speaking literally of a child or of the child within us. I shall always remember the strange face of a young Edinburgh boy, cross-eyed, unwashed and unsure. Like some of the other children from round-about he would come to our community's evening prayer, in part simply for the warmth and quiet of the place. One evening he arrived late. We were already well into a meditation on the icon of the Virgin of Vladimir. 'Our Lady of Tenderness', as she is also called, is portrayed holding the Christ-child in safety and affection. The icon was perched on the mantelpiece by an open fire, and the only place left for the boy to sit was below it on a stool. Maybe because of his eyesight he was unable to see that we were gazing at the icon and not at him. But thinking that *he* was our focus, from that dirty, unbecoming face there came a smile full of the grace of innocence. His countenance became a living icon for us.

What sorts of things do we generally associate with childhood's innocence, and not just in *our* early years but in the infancy, as it were, of all created life? When we think of the young we will think of the way in which they can playfully delight in the moment or amuse themselves in the simplest of ways. We will have images of children dilly-dallying by streams in the countryside or making the most of flowing water in the gutters of a city. We will remember something of the carefree timelessness of our earliest years. Watching a butterfly in the garden, or even an insect slowly making its way across the kitchen floor, will be given all the time in the world. Free from clocks and from any sense of other responsibility, a child will have wonder-filled moments of being totally present to the moment. We hold within us early memories of looking up into open skies, to clouds and the infinite vastness of blue by day and to stars and boundless stretches of space by night, or of lying in the grass feeling its moisture, smelling its greenness, or listening to leaves rustling in the wind.

William Wordsworth, in 'Intimations of Immortality', expresses the belief that if we look far enough back into our childhood we can all bear testimony to this way of seeing that invests every natural object with a type of splendour. He writes:

> There was a time when meadow, grove and stream,
> The earth, and every common sight,
> To me did seem
> Apparelled in celestial light,
> The glory and freshness of a dream.[4]

Although this way of seeing is obscured in us, there is in the embers of our childhood, as he says, 'something that doth live'. It is not utterly abolished or destroyed. While we may have only 'shadowy recollections' of those beginnings, they are the 'master-light of all our seeing'. Even though we cannot return to the innocent experiences of childhood we can uncover within ourselves its way of seeing, enough to know, he says, that each new day 'is lovely yet'.

This sense of wonder at life is a primary experience for us at the earliest stages of our journey. I watched my youngest child lying in his pram under a great fig tree in the garden. He was awake and fully alert but still. He lay watching the sun's light dappling through the intertwined branches and listening to the wind rustling the leaves. After a while he waved his arms at what he was seeing and uttered an appreciative cooing sound. I realized as I watched that this was a universal type of experience, something of which we have all known in the almost entirely faded memories of early childhood. Like Edwin Muir's recollection of one of his earliest memories the picture carries with it a sense of timelessness:

> I was lying in some room watching a beam of slanting light in which dusty, bright motes slowly danced and turned, while a low murmuring went on somewhere, possibly the humming of flies. My mother was in the room, but where I do not know; I was merely conscious of her as a vague, environing presence. This picture is clear and yet indefinite, attached to one summer day at the Bu [Muir's family farm], and at the same time to so many others that it may go back to the day when I first watched a beam of light as I lay in my cradle. The quiet murmuring, the slow, unending dance of the motes, the sense of deep and solid peace, have come back to me since only in dreams. This memory has a different quality from any other memory in my life. It was as if, while I lay

watching that beam of light, time had not yet begun.[5]

The grace of wonderment has been planted deep within us. How do we reclaim it and learn again to gaze at the light of the Mystery that dapples through creation and through our lives?

To reflect on the innocence of our childhood is not to romanticize it, for childhood is also the stage of life that is most focussed on its own needs. A child whose basic requirements are not being met, a baby for instance who is hungry or tired, will complain and cry, just as an infant whose needs are being met, who is secure, and well-rested or at the breast, will express contentment. There is no doubting the state of a little one, and it is expressed physically, audibly and uninhibitedly. Innocence means that there will be no dissimulation. Nothing is hidden away, all is transparent. In the rediscovery of the inner child this will mean an openness of heart in us, seeing the needs and fears that are within us as well as expressing our joys and gladness.

The openness of a child can also mean a readiness to trust and to forgive and accept others in ways that are uncomplicated by the learned prejudices of race and colour and nation. These deepest traits reflect the image of God in us, covered over as they may later be by layers of what is false and destructive. The unguarded openness of a child will mean also, of course, vulnerability to the sort of abuse that desecrates innocence. The frequency of such abuse in our society must lead us to ask how deeply buried is the sense of holy innocence at the heart of each child and at the heart of each one of us. The more cut off we are from our truest centre the more destructive will our behaviour become towards ourselves and one another, both individually and collectively.

To become like a child is of course not to go back to infancy and its childishness, but to move more deeply into who we have been created to be as we go forward on our journey. It is to grow from who we essentially are rather than to live out of the false dimensions or failings of our lives. Recovering our innocence is not an attempt to replicate the behaviour of our infancy. Rather it is to reclaim the grace of innocence that we were given in childhood and to integrate it with the graces that have come to us with later stages of life. To see a wise old man playing peekaboo with his grandson or laughing freely again about the silliest things of life is to know that the child that has always been in him is being liberated once more. It may also be that the grandchild has in part been the agent of that rediscovered freedom in him. The way in which a child loves to hear stories from our own childhood can be the grace that opens up for us again the heart of who we are. What are the things of innocence in us that have been wrongfully pressed down, the simplicity, the wonder and openness, that need to be set free again?

Perhaps it would be a good thing to carry with us throughout life a photograph of ourselves as infants. To look now and again at that child's face and to know that it is at the core of who we are, even though there is now much more to it as well, will be to be reminded of a beauty that is to be recovered. And similarly to look into the faces of our newborn is to be reminded that their innocence has come in part through us and is from that depth within us that bears the likeness of God's image.

Edwin Muir, in his poem 'The Original Place',

speaks of our native land as a good, free and beautiful inheritance. Although it has been threatened from without, and altered to the point of having apparently lost its liberty, Muir writes:

> But at its centre stands
> A stronghold never taken.[6]

Stormed again and again by attack we can yet know the heart of who we have been created to be as held secure by God. We can know that our deepest root still springs from that place. It is not a pretending that the unalloyed purity of innocence would be preferable to the mixture of who we have become as a result of life's experience. Rather it is an allowing the root from that Eden within us to bear fruit that could never have been born in our childhood. As Muir writes in 'One Foot in Eden':

> Strange blessings never in Paradise
> Fall from these beclouded skies.[7]

Grace leads us not backwards but forwards into a redemption of what is truest in us.

Exercise

Sitting comfortably but alert, begin to repeat silently the phrase, 'To such as these belongs the kingdom of God.'

Find a rhythm for the repetition of the words that keeps time with your breathing. Try saying the phrase as you breathe in. Breathe slowly and deeply, allowing the words to fill you before breathing out.

Be conscious that they are being spoken from deep

within. Listen to them as an expression of the Word that was in the beginning and through whom all things are made. Allow them to recollect in you the innocence that was planted at the core of your life. 'To such as these belongs the kingdom of God.' Listen silently for fifteen minutes, allowing the truth of these words to uncover that part of yourself that 'belongs to the kingdom of God'.

In the silence of meditation it is not a matter of thinking about the words but rather of opening yourself to them and allowing them in God's own time and way to bear fruit in your mind and life. If discursive thought does come simply return to a repetition of the phrase as a way of moving deeper than thought, into memory and image and even into a total stillness of mind.

After the fifteen minutes of meditation express your heart's desire in prayer. What is it you most deeply desire in your own life and for the world? Express this longing in prayer before finishing with the Lord's Prayer.

3 ✤ Adolescence and Awakening

'Why were you searching for me?'
(Luke 2.49)

What is it we think of when we recall our adolescence? And what is it that seems most to characterize our teenagers' lives? Perhaps above all else it is a stage in life marked by a huge range of awakenings. We wake up to new thoughts and perspectives on life. We more emphatically form opinions and begin to reflect on the world around us. The fields and the streets in which we played as youngsters without much self-consciousness we now approach with a sense of self, sometimes to the point of an excruciating self-consciousness. We are awakened to new feelings and the stirrings of unfamiliar emotions. And related to this is the birth of sexual awareness and the energies of attraction and new desires for physical and emotional intimacy. As we become more conscious of these thoughts and urges that well up from within, there arise also new hopes and expectations of what we will be and do.

The awakenings of adolescence, because of their sheer volume and intensity, give rise also to confusions and inner turbulence. Despite this they are usually accompanied by strong yearnings for greater independence.

Most of us will remember the excitement, even if combined with fear, of first travelling alone or of beginning, independently of family, a new venture or a new stage of education. We will have memories of being allowed for the first time to take a boat out onto open waters, or to head off alone for a day's expedition into the woods or hills. Similarly, we will remember occasions of being denied a greater independence when we felt ready for it and the frustration, if not clandestine behaviour on our part, that followed such a decision. Jesus' words to his parents, 'Why were you searching for me?', speak of a youth's longings for independence. In St Luke's account the twelve-year-old boy, without permission from his parents, had decided to stay behind in Jerusalem to listen to the teachers in the temple. For three days his parents anxiously searched for Jesus, and upon finally locating him Mary expresses her hurt in the words, 'Why have you treated us like this?' But Jesus' action is based on the beginnings of an awakening within himself of who he is. With this comes a desire to learn and act in a way that will increasingly be separate from that of his parents and their understanding of him. The story is pointing in part to the grace of awakening, in which what has been hidden in the unconscious is raised into consciousness.

St Luke's story conveys something of the awakenings that begin to occur in each one of us in adolescence. At that stage of life we are granted a grace of reflection and an alertness to dimensions of ourselves that before we were unaware of. This of course is not to say that we are given this grace only in adolescence, or that it is in any sense a complete grace of self-knowledge. Far from it! Rather it is to say that aspects of self-awakening come to birth in us most naturally and forcefully during these years. That it might also be combined with naiveté or confusions and contradictions does not detract from the fact that a grace of awakening begins to stir powerfully within us during adolescence.

What is it then that happens to this wakefulness? Do we allow it to remain alive and active, further releasing a sense of self in us, so that more and more we may explore the yet undiscovered depths of who we are? Or do we choose to shut down to the grace of awakening, preferring instead shallower foundations to the structure of what we know to be true about ourselves? In terms of spirituality, the Western world, with its emphatically materialistic way of seeing, has chosen to close itself off to the depths of the mystery. Just as birth is prevalently viewed in narrow biological terms, so life becomes measured in terms of physical appearance and material possession. The perspective that comes across again and again in the scriptural tradition on the other hand is that there are 'great and hidden things', as Jeremiah says, waiting to be made known to us.[1] As we learn to study our inner depths, looking with a telescope, as it were, into the infinity of our own souls, what once seemed hazy collections of disorder will be seen instead to be constellations, 'hidden worlds within worlds', as Coleridge said.[2] The space and infinity of the great stretches of the cosmos are like symbols of the eternal and expansive inner world of our spirits. What are the things that we will come to learn in being awakened to that world within?

The Irish novelist, James Joyce, described one of his characters as living at some distance from himself. If we are not awake to the spiritual depths that are within us, and alert to inner truths that are waiting to be raised into consciousness, then we will live at a distance from our true selves. St Augustine, in his *Confessions*, reflecting on the spiritual journey of his life, and in particular on the years of separation from God, said that it was not that God had been separated from him but rather that he had been separated from himself. 'You were with me, but I was not with you.'[3] To be reconciled to God is to be reconciled to our true self, made as we are in his image. It is to be recollected or united again at the heart of who we have been created to be.

The grace of awakening is one of becoming aware of who we truly are, and choosing to live out of that truth. The story of the father trying to wake his son up for school in the morning makes this point. The son responded to the knocking at his bedroom door by saying, 'I am not going to get up, and I shall tell you three reasons why: the first is because I hate education, the second is because the children tease me, and the third is because education is boring.' To this the father replied, 'You *are* going to get up, and I shall tell you three reasons why: the first is because it is your duty to get up, the second is because you are forty-five years old, and the third is because you are the headmaster.' We need to wake up to who we are.

Not only is it an awakening but a choosing to get up, as it were, or to live according to the truth that has been spoken within us. The grace that enables us to become more aware of who we are is one that can stir also within us the desire to be conformed to that truth. Just as Jesus told the paralysed man who lay on his bed to stand and walk,[4] so there are creativities within us that have not only been undiscovered but unused, and in being unused are underdeveloped, if not entirely seized up. Being awakened to a creative depth will be the initial kindling within us of a desire to be restored or reconnected to that creativity. The grace of awakening is one that can lead us further and further into the truth of who we are. What is it that will so awaken and restore us? Where are we to look or listen?

The ninth-century Irish teacher, John Scotus Eriugena, taught that the Word of God is being forever uttered. If God were to stop speaking, he said, 'the created universe would cease to exist'.[5] Eriugena was saying this in the context of writing a commentary on the prologue to St John's Gospel, and in particular on the words, 'In the beginning was the Word', and 'All things have come into being through the Word'.[6] Our life, and the life of all creation, is essentially an expression of God, an utterance not only from the very beginning of time but from the heart of all time and space. The birth of each child and each creature is an utterance of the One who is at the beginning of life. And so in listening for what will awaken and restore us, we are not listening to an utterance from some religious periphery of life, but rather to the Word that is being uttered at the very heart of who we are and of what life most essentially is. It is the Word that has uttered us into being. It is in hearing this Word that we will be awakened to what is deepest and truest in us.

The awakenings that occur in adolescence are of a tremendous mixture. It is not just truth that we begin to hear within us as adolescents but also uncertainties and false voices that can mislead us as to who we are. It is not just light and streams of good creativity that we glimpse in our inner depths, but great voids of darkness too and selfish and destructive currents. For what we are awakened to in adolescence is an intimation of the complexities of soul that we become more aware of later in life if we continue to listen. The gospel is given not to suddenly erase from us the interplay between light and darkness, or between truth and what is false, but to undergird us with a deep assurance that the light has not been overcome by the darkness.[7] It is given that we may know the hidden truth, that deeper than any falseness in us is the truth of God's image at the heart of who we are. It is given to enable us to name and confront the destructive energies that are within, in the certainty that stronger still are the redemptive graces of God's life planted at the core of who we are.

On the island of Patmos, where St John the Divine in his Revelation saw forces of darkness emerging from an abyss that seemed limitless in its reserve,[8] there is a cave that was traditionally associated with evil. People who entered it were said never to appear again. In the early Christian era a hermit monk settled in that part of the island. For years he lived and prayed within sight of the cave. Then he moved to its mouth and for another number of years prayed in the face of the evil of that place. Finally he entered the cave itself and took up residence. The cave was redeemed. This in part is a story that points to being alert to the darknesses that are hidden within, and to how it is that we are to face them. It is a story also that points to the confidence, but not naiveté, with which we can confront evil.

The fourteenth-century English mystic, Julian of Norwich, saw in one of her 'Revelations of Divine Love', that her soul was like an eternal world. And seated on a throne at the heart of that world was Jesus, 'beautiful in person, great in stature'. She saw that he would never leave the place that he holds in our souls. 'For in us is he completely at home,' she said, 'and has his eternal dwelling.'[9] Again and again in Julian's vision is the conviction that while our perception of that centre is often obscured, it is the deepest reality of life. The Word that was in the beginning and will be in the end, and which is being uttered continuously from the heart of life, is first and foremost the Word of Love, terrifying and mysterious as it may also be to us.

If that is the deepest utterance, why is it that so often we prefer *not* to be further awakened and not to listen to what is beneath the surface? In part it is because of the disturbing and even destructive things that we may hear within, the shadow side of our selves. And related to this, will it not also be that in listening we will be called to change? A determined old Scot was asked in his nineties how it was that he had remained so single-minded. 'I have remained single-minded', he said, 'by being stone deaf.' If we do not hear what is being said, and in particular if we do not hear the Word that is being uttered from the very heart of life, then we will not have to adapt our lives to a reality other than the one we fancy to be true.

In adolescence there is a turbulent awakening to new dimensions and characteristics of ourselves, both good and bad. These can be unsettling and demanding. Think of the tortuous feelings that an adolescent can go through with the first stirrings of love, combined as they will sometimes be with rejection. Many of us will remember the sheer intensity of lines of adolescent poetry in which we or others tried to give expression to the realizations coming to birth in us. Often this is caricatured as mere self-absorption. There may of course be an overindulgence in self-attention, but in the main what is happening is such a powerful flood of awakening that it can be difficult for the adolescent to take his eyes off it.

Some of us probably need to ask ourselves why it is

at times that we have become so annoyed with the self-focus of our adolescents, when it seems that they are aware of no one but themselves. This shadow-side of the adolescent can produce a strong reaction in us. Why is that? Is it entirely because of our belief in the importance of them learning to become aware of others? Might it not reflect also a frustration in us about not finding enough time for ourselves, or not giving ourselves to a greater discipline of self-awareness? And if we have remained insufficiently open to the grace of awakening in our lives, we may well at some level regret this and project some of our frustration onto the self-discovering adolescent. This of course becomes more complicated if the reason we have closed down to further awareness in ourselves is because waking up has created in us the type of turbulence and inner confusion that we witness in an adolescent.

In a similar vein, is some of the hostility and prejudice that we find in parts of the Western world towards forms of meditation, for instance, not rooted in the same type of inner frustration about a lack of self-awakening? How often have we heard those who pursue a discipline of meditation and silence described as 'navel gazing'? Of course it is right to be wary about a tendency towards self-preoccupation. And we need always to be reminded that Christian meditation is not about moving away from the life of the world, but about stepping more deeply into an awareness of the One who is the very Life of the world's life. But is that where the heat of any prejudice against meditation really comes from? We each need to be asking ourselves if we are finding the right balance between inner awakening and outer awareness. That, more than commenting on the intriguing imbalances of others, is of the first importance.

Our concern ought to be that in being awakened within we hear what is true, rather than simply hearing what we fancy or fear to be true. There is the story of the old couple, Jock and Mary, who celebrated their sixtieth wedding anniversary. At the end of the long day of festivities, sitting at home together, Jock took Mary's hand and said to her, 'Mary, I am proud of you.' Mary's hearing not being what it once was, she said, 'What was that, Jock?' 'I am proud of you,' said Jock again; to which Mary replied, 'That's all right Jock, I'm tired of you too.'

It is important that we hear what is really being said, and most important of all is to hear the Word that is being uttered from the heart of life, of our lives and all life. In becoming alert within we will hear many things, and some of what we hear will be born not of the truth that is within us but rather of the fears or hatreds that may be in us. There are places in our souls that are haunted by the self-doubts and failures of our lives. They correspond in darkness to some of the most frightening outward places of death in our world. And the words of confusion or rage that issue from such inner chambers do not come from the Heart of life but from peripheries that obscure the deepest and eternally life-giving Word.

The risks attached to continuing to be awakened to new births within us are great. For who knows what will emerge in us next and what the infinitely creative and imaginative Spirit of God will allow us to see and call us to do? Far from being allowed to be settled, we may be given the impatience of a youth to burst out of the traditional boundaries that we have inherited, especially if those boundaries threaten to limit the depth and breadth of our awakening. Or it may be the sharpness of a youth's sight that we will be given to see through the irrelevancies and hypocrisies of our religious traditions. One of the risks of awakening is that of entering periods of doubting what we have received. Do most of us not remember as adolescents the need to know and prove things for ourselves, and the tendency to doubt until we saw with our own eyes? Let us have the confidence, both for ourselves and for our youngsters, not to close down to doubt but to move through it to what is deeper, and that is faith.

Is this not part of the grace of awakening? And need we be frightened by it? If our adolescents are being awakened to new thought and reflective ability should we not be making room for them, as well as for us, to doubt as part of the journey towards more fully believing? Is this not in part the truth of Jesus' story of the prodigal son,[10] whose full awakening happens only through a time of questioning and rejecting what was his? The son who takes the risk of following his doubts, before awakening to the deeper truth of who he is and who his father is, becomes the son of much greater spiritual stature than the one who never left home. Let us not so much fear the risks and wanderings of our doubts as believe in the One who waits for us and for our children to return home in an awakened and more deeply alert state of soul. As one old Greek woman told me in speaking with affection of her wayward son, 'The Church loves a good sinner.' In her words there was the clear impression that a place would always be kept for him, and that on his return his presence would be celebrated with a joy much greater than if he had never gone astray. Let us know that the deep awakenings of life in us are a gift, shrouded as they will often be in years of confusion and pain, both for ourselves and for those whom our lives touch.

In her *Revelations of Divine Love*, Julian of Norwich saw that all will be well. "'All things shall be well'," she had been assured. "'You shall see for yourself that all manner of thing shall be well".'[11] This she believed not on the basis of some vague optimism about life and its endings, for she had seen too the woundedness and terrible disfigurement of life that Christ's sufferings represent. Rather she believed these words of promise because she had seen the One who is at the eternal centre of our souls. She had seen the Mother who will not cease to wait for our return home. 'Why were you anxiously searching for me?', asks Jesus. The deepest awakenings in us are stirrings of love to draw us to the heart of who we are.

Exercise

At the end of this Gospel story Mary is described as treasuring 'all these things in her heart' (Luke 2.51). Although she had been frustrated and even hurt by Jesus' awakening to a new consciousness of himself, she comes to ponder and treasure this event. Mary's response can guide us in meditating on the graces of awakening in our own lives.

Finding a comfortable but alert sitting position, begin to repeat silently the words, 'Treasure these things in your heart.' The phrase can be abbreviated further into a simple, 'Treasure these things.'

Discover a rhythm for the repetition that allows the words to be spoken simply and directly to your own heart. It may be that saying them as you breathe down will allow you to listen to the words from within. Pause after your breath to allow the words to settle within you. Then, as you breathe upwards, memories and images of awakening may arise. On the other hand, it may be simply a quiet sense of the presence of God that you are given. This, perhaps above all else, is the awakening to be sought and treasured.

After approximately fifteen minutes of silent meditation begin to express your heart's desires to God, both for yourself and for those whom God has given you to care for and delight in. Extend these prayerful desires for people everywhere. Finish with the Lord's Prayer.

4 ✦ Early Adulthood and Passion

'My house shall be a house of prayer'
(Luke 19.46)

Do we remember the passionately held certainties of young adulthood, what Chesterton sarcastically called 'the towering infallibility of twenty'? They may not always have been matured convictions, and in calling the world to change we may sometimes simply have been calling the world to become more like us, but they will have had often a true fire of passion about them. The acute sense of wrong and injustice in the world and the determination to do something about it issue from what the Scriptures call the very bowels of compassion. These are the words used to describe Jesus' passion for feeding the hungry,[1] for instance, or his outpouring of mercy for the widow who had lost her only son.[2] Compassion is fuelled by a fire in the heart. The motivation that wells up from deep within us to protest against inequity, for example, to work for peace or to call the Church to its original simplicity are reflections of some of the heartfelt idealism that emerges in early adulthood. What is this grace of passion for life that comes to the fore in these years? Have we cherished it and continued to give it room in our lives, individually and collectively, or are we a bit frightened by its strength and unpredictability?

In St Luke's account of the triumphal entry into Jerusalem, Jesus is described as weeping over the city because it has not known, as he says, 'the things that make for peace'.³ And on entering the temple and witnessing the exploitation of the poor whereby they were being charged inflated prices for sacrificial offerings, Jesus violently overturns the tables of money changers and drives out the temple merchants with a whip of cords. In the great tradition of Old Testament prophets, Jesus denounces injustice and at the same time affirms the sacredness of the holy place by quoting from the prophet Isaiah, 'My house shall be a house of prayer.'⁴

The Hebrew prophets often used the passionate language of love and intimacy to represent the relationship of God to the people. 'I have loved you with an everlasting love,' as Jeremiah writes;⁵ or 'How can I give you up?', exclaims Hosea.⁶ These phrases resonate with our experiences of being almost possessed by love at times in our lives. Have we not all known something of the passion for another in which a part of our heart is forever captured? We will remember the excitement and fervour of first moments of love, as we will remember also the excruciating pain of being betrayed in love or rejected. This depth of passionate relationship will often have first come to birth in us in early adult years. Why is it given us and how are we to integrate it into the rest of our lives?

It is important, of course, that we be clear as to what true passion is about. We can be terribly confused in the focus and the expression of our passions. H. A. Williams, in his autobiographical account of his search for God, entitled *Some Day I'll Find You*,[7] describes his mother's practice of holding prayer meetings in her living room. On one occasion late in life, when she was halfway through reading the American classic *Gone with the Wind*, she passionately prayed that Scarlet O'Hara would make the right decision. We have the capacity to love deeply and truly. We are capable also of ridiculously missing the point at times.

Part of the misplacing of passion in our Western world is the degree to which we focus exclusively on its sexual manifestations. The response to this from the religious community has been to deny far too often the essential goodness of sexual passion and delight. There has been a tendency, for instance, to spiritualize a book like the Song of Songs, one of the most sensuous pieces of literature in the Judeo-Christian tradition. Its passionate love poetry, while pointing to an unquench-able passion that is stronger than death and therefore greater than the physical, does not neglect at the same time to give place to the sexual expression of passion. The denial of the latter has had the effect of repressing energies that issue from deep within who we have been created to be. At the heart of life is a great rhythm of passion that expresses itself in longings for unity in and between all things.

There is the story of a headmistress warning her schoolgirls that an hour of pleasure is not worth an eternity of regret. In response one of the girls raised her hand and said, 'Please Miss, how do you make the pleasure last for so long?' This is precisely the question that needs to be asked. Passion, at its outward level, does not last, even though it may be obsessively pur-sued for a lifetime. The response to limited notions of passion should not be a denying of the sexual but of confidently moving deeper than the sexual to be aware of the passion for life that can be awakened at the heart of who we are. To once know the strength and goodness of that grace is to begin to set in perspective the various outward expressions of it. Deep inner passion is like a mighty river that flows into many streams. The sexual is but one stream and it may not necessarily be pursued, but if it is let us celebrate it as a rich and deep stream. Let us also know, however, that it is narrow. It will flow truly only when bounded by the banks of commitment. One of the greatest modern fallacies is that the stream of sexual passion can be both deep and unbounded.

Jesus' cleansing of the temple expressed his depth of inner passion. This was no superficial religious concern. Its parallel today is not a fastidious protectiveness of our church sanctuaries from all noise and liveliness. Rather the Mystery that was guarded in the half-light of the temple, and the love of God that was taught in the Scriptures and ritual of the sacred place, pointed to the Holiness and the Love that are at the heart of all life. Jesus' outrage was motivated not by a liturgical fanaticism for decorum in the temple but by a passionate desire to reclaim an awareness and a reverence for the One who dwells in the inner sanctuary of the Temple of Life itself. Let us be passionate about recovering a sense of space and stillness in our holy places, but in doing so let us know that at heart we are pointing to the stillness within ourselves and within all life that needs to be rediscovered. What are the temples, what are the places in our lives and in our world that need to be cleared out, uncluttered of all that opposes or obstructs our awareness of God's presence?

Physically our churches, if they are in a state of clutter,

will speak of a lack of space and stillness. The sometimes absurd hoarding of bits and pieces from the past,
with sanctuaries strewn with unnecessary furnishings
and a confusing assortment of papers and books, can
convey an absence of inner composure. It may be that
what is needed in many places is for most of our
religious paraphernalia, including the great fixed pews
of many sanctuaries, to be thrown out of our church
doors. We need to recover simplicity and uncluttered
attentiveness. Think of the way, for instance, in which a
bedroom will be prepared with nesting instinct before
the arrival of a newborn child. Cleaned, freshly painted
and uncluttered it is a symbol of waiting and welcome.
Simplified and focussed places of silence and prayer
will similarly speak of the yearnings in us to receive the
life that is born from within.

More important than rooms and buildings are our
minds and bodies, which as St Paul said are living
temples of God.[8] What are the distractions or obses-
sions that need to be cleared out if we are to be more
aware of the silent mystery of God within us and
within the body of creation? Jesus' teaching in relation
to the practice of prayer was to 'go into your room and
shut the door and pray to your Father who is in secret,
and your Father who sees in secret will reward you'.[9]
At one level these words point literally to the importance of physical spaces in which we may pray without
external distraction. At an even deeper level they speak
of the need to close the doors of our minds from dis-
tracting thoughts that crowd in upon us and lead us
who knows where. The great traditions of prayer and
meditation that have been passed down over the centuries provide us with simple ways in which to focus
the attention of our spirits. They offer practical methods

of learning to 'be still', as the psalmist says, in order to
know God.[10] As the modern Scottish poet, Kenneth
White, expresses it in his poem, 'The House of Insight',
it is a 'taking off the clothes of the mind' and 'making
love to the unknown':

> multiple meditations
> the wonderful understanding
> wunderstanding
> into the nakedness
> behind the signs
> deep deep down
> where it all
> ultimately matters . . .
> surrounded by eternity[11]

Similarly in the temple of our homes how is it that we
can free our family dwellings in the midst of their
busyness at the same time to be open and attentive
places, uncluttered by anxieties and the distractions that
crowd out an experience of well-being at their heart?
This in part is what Mahatma Gandhi was attempting
in his Hindu ashram when he designed his own
dwelling to be as simple and open as possible. The inner
discipline of stillness is one that can be aided by freeing
ourselves from the outward clutter of things. Among
my enduring memories of Bede Griffiths, one of the
greatest spiritual teachers of the twentieth century, was
the open simplicity of his hut in the Indian Benedictine
community of Shantivanam in Tamil Nadu. As Bede sat
in his bed, physically weakened by a recent stroke, his
eyes conveyed a passionately alive clarity of spirit,
something of which was reflected in the openness of
his room, windows wide open to the light and breeze
of the day. Jesus said, 'Blessed are the pure in heart for

they will see God.'[12] In all the temples of life, whether that be the temple of our hearts or the temple of creation itself, how do we regain this pure and uncluttered vision of the presence of the Sacred?

'If the doors of perception were cleansed,' wrote Blake, 'every thing would appear to man as it is, infinite.'[13] Our inner eyes need to catch fire, he said, if we are to see God. Against what may appear overwhelming odds, given the inner and outer distractions of our lives, how are we to recover a visionary way of seeing unless our passion is set alight? In fact what is it of value in any aspect of life that happens without the flame of passion? St John the Divine records in his book of Revelation that the One who is the beginning of creation says to the angel of the church in Laodicea, 'Because you are lukewarm, and neither cold nor hot, I am about to spit you out of my mouth.'[14] If we do not feel passionate about one another, for instance, or about what it is we are doing or studying or creating together, what will happen? Surely it is no coincidence that the gift of passion between a man and a woman is what gives rise to conception and life. Similarly the passion that exists in an artist, the passion of a mother for her child, or the passion in a people to be freed from oppression, and all the day-to-day passions of interest in work and play and relationship is what gives rise to creativity and new beginnings in our lives. What are the passions of faith and of hope, and above all, what are the passions of love that are waiting to be rediscovered in our lives and in the Church and world?

We live in an age that increasingly sees through a passionless and tame religiosity. As the prophetic figure George MacLeod used to say about much twentieth-century religion, 'The problem with the Church is that

51

no one wants to persecute it.' Has it lost its fire of passion? If prayer is at the heart of a spirituality that sets out to transform our lives and the world, then the lack of energy and discipline around practices of inner awareness and strength speaks of a passionless devotion. Another fiery Celtic saint of Iona, the sixth-century St Columba, instructed his monastic community to pray until the tears come.[15] Most of us will recall moments in our lives when we have been threatened by a fear of losing what we hold most dear, our children, our partner, our loved ones. In such moments we have prayed with passion and perhaps also with tears. A passionate spirituality is one that is awakened by such depths of longing. It is passionately alert to the temples of God being threatened in the world, whether they be the temples of innocent lives, the inner temples of our hearts, or the garden temples of creation.

Established religion has tended historically to be frightened by prophetic passion, portrayed often as born in the wild places of desert or open sea. The passionate voice of Old Testament prophets rages into the city like a storm from the wilderness. 'I hate, I despise your festivals, and I take no delight in your solemn assemblies,' says the prophecy of Amos. 'Instead let justice roll down like waters, and righteousness like an everflowing stream.'[16] The passion of God that is expressed in prophetic cries for justice is a passion uttered also in the wildness of God's creativity. The strength of the waves of the sea, the immense explosive energies of the stars, and the lack of neat straight lines in all that grows from the ground, speak of an unbounded wildness of passion in God. This is the passion at the heart of life and at the heart of our true selves. It is a grace that arouses in us a longing for the unity and integration of all things.

In a group meditation on this Gospel text a woman spoke of having seen herself as a wild, red rose, covered and bound by weeds. In stripping them away she saw her hands badly cut but continued to tear them away because in so doing she knew that her true self was being uncovered. It is like the great west window of St Giles' Cathedral in Edinburgh, dedicated to the memory of the Scottish poet Robert Burns, and inspired by the words of his poem, 'My love is like a red, red rose'. At the heart of the window is the red flower or flame, an image of the love that is at the heart of life. The realm of creation and the world of humanity are depicted as streaked through with terribly dark lines of wrong and confusion, but deeper still are the strands of golden light that issue from the rose and are interwoven through all things. At the centre of life and at its beginning is the fire of passion.

Let us be assured that our deepest passions are good and of God. Yes, of course there are other desires in us as well, selfish and destructive, but deeper still is the passion of love, for we are made in the image of the One who is self-giving love. The gospel is given not primarily to tell us that many of our passions are dark and destructive, for we more or less know that about ourselves. Rather the truth which we have forgotten and which the gospel is given to recall us to, and thus to liberate us with, is that we bear within ourselves the passion and creativity of God. It is the wild creative passion of the One whose explosion of energy and matter in the beginning gave birth to the expanding cosmos. Grace is given to release that creative passion from our depths and to free us from the powers of lethargy and destructiveness that obscure what is truest in us as sons and daughters of God.

A deep awakening of passion in us is something that will stir into life the passion that is in others too. True passion however will invite rather than force response. 'Love bade me welcome', as Herbert wrote.[17] The deepest passion will kindle into awakening what is truest in the other. The repulsive image conversely of a man sexually forcing himself on a woman speaks of the perversion of passion and the altering of an energy that is essentially good and life-giving into something that is destructive. The extent to which there is domination and abuse sexually in our culture speaks of the depth to which the image of God's passion in us has been covered over by what is false. True passion is one that desires to release love above all else and thereby set the other free.

When Jesus expressed passion in the Jerusalem temple in order to free it as a place of prayer, he moved closer to that other passion, the suffering of the cross. As a result of his action St Luke tells us that the religious leadership began to make plans to kill him. Later as Jesus was being led to crucifixion, and women witnessing it were beating their breasts and wailing, Jesus said in relation to the sufferings that would come to the holy city, 'Daughters of Jerusalem, do not weep for me, but weep for yourselves and for your children.'[18] He spoke as a man who had openly shown his own depth of emotion, not only in the temple, but earlier when he had wept at the death of his friend,[19] and then over a city whose turmoil of confusion was bringing destruction on itself.[20] His words to the women of Jerusalem point to the importance of expressing the passions that move most deeply within us. As the psychiatrist Elizabeth Kuebler Ross emphasized exaggeratedly in her work with the dying and the bereaved, 'Expressed anger lasts for exactly twenty seconds. Unexpressed anger', she said, 'lasts a life time.' We know, do we not, even when tears come to our eyes through laughter and delight, let alone through pain and anger, that something has stirred within us at depths far beneath the surface. The conscious integration of those inner depths is part of the journey towards wholeness.

The way in which the word 'passion' points both to love and to suffering is reflective of the mystery of Christ. And perhaps this in part is why we so often choose to inhibit or bury our deepest passions. We know how costly they are. Even our more superficial passions are demanding, let alone our truest ones. To express ourselves in love to another, for instance, is to lay ourselves bare. It is to drop our protective barriers and be exposed to the vulnerability of either receiving love in return or being rejected. Similarly to give ourselves passionately to a creative work or to our children or a movement for liberation is at times to throw caution to the wind. Passion may appear to take us near the edge but it is also the grace that moves us closer to the centre of life. To follow it is in a sense to be willing to die to the outer layers of self-protection so that a new thing may be born in us. From without it may appear madness. From within it is inspiration.

There are fears in us all about such loss of control in life. Of course we need to remember that one of the fruits of the Spirit is self-control.[21] Some of the most powerful forces for good in the world have been men and women who have sustained their passion for justice or for creativity by combining it with disciplined restraint. But in another sense the decision to follow our God-given passions will expose us to being out of control. That was the cost of Christ's loving. Are we expecting it to be entirely different in our own? Jesus said in relation to those who wanted to be his followers, 'Let them take up their cross daily and follow me.'[22]

One woman in meditating on this Gospel story saw herself as a dead caterpillar sitting on a branch. For most of her life, she said, her passions had been cocooned, both by family and by traditional expectations of how she should behave. Coming to life in her now was a desire to liberate what was deepest and truest. What are the passions that are waiting to be released in us, as individuals and families, as churches and societies? In choosing to let go to the great well-spring of passion within, and knowing that in doing so we may make ourselves vulnerable, let us be assured of both the warning and the promise of Christ. As Jesus went on to say in the following verses of that same chapter of St Luke's Gospel, 'Those who want to save their life will lose it, and those who lose their life for my sake will save it.'[23] Pray God that we will have the courage to lose ourselves to the passions of love and creativity that stir deep within us.

Exercise

It is important that you be both still and alert in meditation. Sit, either on a chair or the floor, with your back straight, and begin to repeat silently within yourself the words of Jesus in the temple, 'My house shall be a house of prayer.'

Speak the words as you breathe in. Feel the passion that is in them. Listen to them as an expression of the Life that is within your life. Allow them to be your words. As you breathe out be aware of the stillness that Jesus' words and actions long for. It is the stillness at the heart of life and of creativity.

Memories and images of passion will be called forth by these words. Allow them to flow into your consciousness without stopping to analyse them. It may be that you would like to think about them later, but for now simply be aware of them. Be present to the memories and images as they are given to you or to the sense of peace as you experience it.

After fifteen minutes of silently repeating the words, express your heart's desires in prayer. They may be desires that have been freshly awakened during meditation or they may be desires of which you have been long aware. Whatever they are, whether great or small, know that your deepest desires issue up from God's image within you and can be uttered in prayer. Finish by saying the Lord's Prayer.

5 ✤ Middle Years and Commitment

———ᴧᴧᴧᴧ₨₨◉₨₨ᴧᴧᴧᴧ———

'Love one another as I have loved you'
(John 15.12)

What are our memories of being loved? Who are the people who cared for us in our childhood and have been committed to us at different stages of our journey? Early on it will have been our mothers and fathers, or maybe aunts and uncles or grandparents. These are the ones we will remember, but before them there stretch generations of mothers and fathers in whom patterns of loving have been developed. We tend to love as we have been loved. As well as the way in which we care for one another in families there are patterns of humour and perspective or style of affection and relationship that are passed from one generation to the next. The opposite of course is also true. Patterns of neglect and violence can similarly be inherited.

St Augustine in his *Confessions* speaks of us carrying within ourselves a storehouse or sanctuary of memory. In it is all we have experienced or learned in life, all we have seen and sensed. There is, he says, for each specific memory a gateway that needs to be opened if the recollection of it is to be brought into the present. Sometimes memories from our childhood will come bursting out of such gateways, almost of their own accord. At other times we need to work hard at summoning them and intentionally drawing them forth. Deeper even than memories of what we have experienced and learned, he says, are memories hidden away in the soul's deepest recesses.[1] From these depths come a type of memory that does not depend on our individual life experience or learning. Almost anticipating modern notions of the subconscious, or 'unconscious', Augustine was pointing to an inner connection with what has gone before. Modern science describes this in terms of the whole of life, both past and present, being like a web of interdependent relationships. And new physics, as well as new psychology, even go so far as to say that the life and consciousness that are within us are an unfolding of what was 'contained' in the initial explosion of matter.[2] The origins of the universe are in a sense present within all of us. What has gone before lives in us still.

We do not know everything that has preceded us in our families. We may have a sense, although even here it may only be a fleeting impression, of how the kindness of a grandmother for instance lives on in us as a source of strength and stability in our lives. But before her there were generations, and even millennia, of men and women whose acts of love form the root of much of what we are. There been generations of men sweating hard in the fields and women toiling at their work, in part simply out of a commitment to care for their families. There have been tender and passionate expressions between husband and wife, and conception and pain of birth, again all part of the stream of life that flows through us now. Similarly there are the wrongs and faithlessness and cruelties of the past that also have a place in the inner memory of our lives. These affect the way we love or fail to love.

Edwin Muir, in his poem 'The Journey Back', speaks of the importance of seeking out those who have gone before in order to know the ones through whom the river of life has flowed to us:

> Seek the beginnings, learn from whence you came,
> And know the various earth of which you are made.[3]

In one sense of course we cannot know a great deal about them, nor can we gather much detail about the spirit in which they lived and loved. At another level though there can be the important consciousness that we carry in our lives something of their life, and that their influence, both good and bad, still exerts itself deep within us.

How is it then that we learn to love and in some cases reverse the cycle of destructive patterns received from the past? In addition to the unconscious influences within us, we learn in large part through example and through choice. Memories of our parents hugging behind the kitchen counter, for example, remain indelibly with us from childhood, as do times of argument and family discord. Children love to hear stories of what their parents did when they were younger and how they first met and loved. It is as if they are rehearsing within themselves patterns of how they will choose to live and love. In St John's Gospel it is after Jesus has washed the disciples' feet that he says to them, 'Love one another as I have loved you.' He invites them to follow his example.

Even in creation we find a memory or instinct of

how to love or care being passed from one generation to the next. Images abound from the natural world of birds busily feeding their young or of one generation after another of mother bear ferociously defending her cubs. We know such instincts in ourselves as well, in relation to our children and family. What is the relationship between these natural patterns of protectiveness and the call of Christ to love as we have been loved?

There has been a tendency in Western Christianity to divide the Creator from the Redeemer, and therefore nature from grace. While creation is acknowledged as gift from God, it is at the same time viewed as essentially flawed. Grace therefore is seen not as co-operating with what is natural but as opposed to it. The New Testament on the other hand holds creation and grace in a tension of relationship. Christ is the One 'in whom all things have been made',[4] and so all that has been made is essentially good. At the same time Christ is described as the One who 'sets us free from the law of sin',[5] and so our goodness is seen as bound or oppressed. The desire for love and commitment are rooted deep in the image in which we have been made. When we are unloving and faithless we are being false to our truest self. Deeper than any failing however is the image of God in us and the desire to love. It may be so covered over as to appear lost, but it is there. Grace is given that we may recover this depth and be true to it. Christ's redemptive work is one of saving us from what is false and setting us free to be true to ourselves. If the Church were to regain this perspective, then, instead of being seen so often as opposed to what is natural, its ministry of word and sacrament could be viewed as liberating what we most truly are. This is not to be naive concerning evil's powers of distortion.

Rather it is to believe that deeper than such falseness is the truth of what is in us. Grace is given that we may return to ourselves.

The grace of commitment is one that stirs most powerfully in us during the middle years of life. It is a gift that awakens the desire to seek ways of sustaining relationship and life together. It kindles in us the desire to be committed to marriage and family, for instance, or to work and wider relationship and responsibility. It does not of course come in a vacuum but in the context of the graces that we have already received. In childhood we will often have responded with a purity of intention to situations of need. I remember my son, upon meeting black ANC students from South Africa and hearing their stories of struggle, deciding to write a letter to President de Klerk. It said very simply, 'Stop the hurting'. The grace of commitment is given that we may build on such purity of desire. It is given that we may apply ourselves to working for it. Similarly in relation to the awakenings of adolescence or the passions of young adulthood, the grace of commitment is given that we may serve or extend the goodness of what has already emerged in us. In earlier years we may have been kind and generous when we felt like being so, or when the environment was conducive. In middle life however there come moments of much more intentionally having to choose whether we are going to be committed or uncommitted, to our children and partners or in our workplaces and society or to the deepest truths within us.

A commitment to the truth within us is a starting point for being committed to the truth that is in others as well. 'Love your neighbour as yourself,' says

Jesus.[6] To be unaware of what is within us, or to be neglectful of it, will be to undermine our own attempts at loving others. If we are not alert to the Self who is within our self and all selves, what will the extent of our self-giving be? This of course is not to say that we ever arrive at a sufficient awareness of the Self of God within. Rather it is to say that in giving time and attention to such awareness we will grow in our understanding of the sacredness that is in others. Not that it is only sacredness that we come to know within, but also confusion and shame. The discipline and enduring satisfaction however of becoming reconnected to our true self will kindle further in us the desire and determination to be committed to others.

The decision to be committed, which is a response to the gift of love, is freely chosen. Once it is made however there is the discipline of love, the being committed when we do not necessarily feel like it. Getting up in the middle of the night for the fifth time to attend to an unsettled child involves choice. Being patient and understanding with family or friends when they frustrate or disappoint us calls for a conscious act of the will. Similarly being faithful in any relationship, whether that be to our partners, our communities or to creation itself, involves making a decision and choosing to renew our commitment. This all begins to make commitment sound a hard task, which in part it is. But deciding again and again for truth and for love bears its own fruit, even when the issue to which we may be committed, such as making peace or creating a just society, seems unsuccessful at the outward level. A faithful response to the grace of commitment, whatever the outcome, nurtures in us a strength and endurance of character that are not easily measured. Let us know however that in following this grace we are being restored to our truest selves.

If the desire to be committed is in the first place born out of love, then it is important to find ways of being recalled to the freshness of our love. Otherwise commitment becomes an onerous duty rather than a fulfilment of what is deepest in us. St John the Divine sees that at the heart of God is love, deeper than the tribulations that he is also author of. The One who is the Beginning and the End commends the church in Ephesus for their commitment to faithful work and perseverance. 'But I have this against you,' he says, 'that you have abandoned the love you had at first. Remember then from what you have fallen.'[7]

How are we to keep alive the strength of love's decision to be committed whatever may happen, for to love one another will lead us through suffering as well as joy? There is the pain of a mother holding her dying child, and knowing that her years of commitment to the child have only increased the pain that she now feels in losing her. The same can be said in the midst of any loss where there has also been commitment, whether that be in relationship or in inner creativity. How did those, for instance, who persevered for years in the fight to free South Africa from apartheid renew the vitality of their commitment in the face of so many setbacks?

In part was it not because they knew how to celebrate their commitment as well as work for it? The images of crowds dancing and singing in the midst of knowing also the cost of endurance points to the way in which the well-springs of commitment can be kept open in us. Whether in our inner lives of prayer or in our personal or collective relationships we need to return again and again to the delight that is at the heart of commitment if we are to sustain the works of love.

It is not only in situations of loss and continued struggle that the grace of commitment needs to be renewed. It is also in the midst of failure, when we have let others down or they us. Maybe the greatest pain in failed relationship comes out of the shattering of our expectations. We need to ask why it is that we think others are not going to fail us in one way or another. Why have we been so shaken at points in our lives by failure of commitment to us or to some common purpose? Do we not know within ourselves that all of us, to greater or lesser extents, have failed in love? To place all our faith in the hope that certain others are never going to fail us is to build on shaky foundations. The realization that as we have failed in love, so, to varying degrees, others also fail, should free us to ask the question as to where ultimately our security in love does lie. If we claim that it is in our husband or wife, or mother or father or friend or admirer, we will all at some level and at some stage be disappointed. The perspective that runs through the Scriptures is that God alone is the unfailing Lover of our souls. 'Even if my mother and father forsake me,' says the psalmist, 'the Lord will take me up.'[8]

The sixteenth-century Spanish Christian mystic, Teresa of Avila, in her great work *The Interior Castle*, saw that there are many rooms within that we may enter in prayer. Some are frightening and seem haunted by doubts and failures. But at the heart of the interior castle is what she calls 'the presence chamber'.[9] There God forever dwells and invites us to enter. It is like a love chamber or nuptial room in which the One who is Love desires to be reunited with us at the heart of who we are. We may have forgotten the way to that room, and it may be that we will not fully enter it this side of death. But the intimations uttered from that place are of God's everlasting affection for us. To hear something of those intimations is to know the love in which we are forever secure.

There will have been people in our lives who have borne something of that unfailing love to us, men and women who have been like living icons of God's affection. Some of that love will have come to us through our friends and lovers, although nearly always with a generous mixture of failings as well. But now and again in life there will have been grandmothers, for instance, or saintly men and women here and there, who have communicated without any selfishness the love for us that was in the beginning and will be in the end. Such people will have made us feel that we are forever cherished, as indeed we are. As unlikely as it often seems that we can convey something of that to others in our lives, let us be alert to the opportunities we are given to be bearers of such unfailing affection. That is often the mark of an older person's relationship with those much younger.

A old man recounted an example of such a relationship from childhood. He had made a terrible mess on freshly painted walls in the family home. When his father returned and found the child's grandmother quietly washing down the walls he asked crossly if the boy had done this. The grandmother replied, 'Would a grandson of mine do such a thing?' It is like the story of a girl and her grand-aunt. Whenever things became difficult for her at home she would scurry along the pathway to the old aunt's house, where a place was especially kept for her. Even if the aunt was away the room was unlocked, and hanging in the room's corner above a bed was a basket of little treats known only to the girl and her grand-aunt. It is in such people that we will have glimpsed something of the unconditional love of God. Like the father in the parable of the prodigal son, it is a love that knows the wrong we have done, but looking deeper than the wrong it waits with desire for our return. This is the One who in creation generously gives sun and rain to both the just and unjust,[10] and whose unfathomable depth of mercy is reflected in Christ's words from the cross, 'Forgive them for they do not know what they are doing.'[11]

How can we so love? The people who have communicated something of this love to us will be people who in a sense have taken their eyes off themselves. No longer are they having to prove themselves, nor are they striving to get ahead. What has produced such confidence in them to love unconditionally? Is it not a knowledge that they are deeply loved, and even that, combined with failings, they are lovable? In the case of Jesus it was a certainty of being loved by God and a confidence that he bore within himself the beauty of the image of God. 'I and the Father', he said, 'are one.'[12] Jesus' words of self-unity with God point to what is most deeply true for us as well. To begin to know such a unity at the heart of who we are is more and more to be set free from the need to focus on ourselves. It is to begin to know a freedom from the bondage of forever seeking the approval of others.

During an afternoon siesta at the Benedictine community of Shantivanam in southern India, I dreamt that a woman of great beauty came to me and said, 'My mother tells me that I have always loved you.' This simple dream raised into consciousness for me in a personal way a new sense of love's depths. Whether the mysterious words point to the love that has come to me through the mystical body of the Church or to the sense of love that has issued up for me from the unconscious, the dream in its simplicity spoke also of a universal truth. We are, each one, loved at the core of our beings. It is the knowledge of this truth that can set us free to love one another as we are loved.

Exercise

Sitting in a comfortable but alert position, begin to repeat silently the words of Jesus, 'Love one another as I have loved you.'

Allow the repetition of the words to keep time with your breathing. As you breathe upwards, say, 'Love one another.' Let the words issue from deep within, rising up into your full attention. They are spoken by the One who is the beginning and the end, and who dwells at the heart of life. As you breathe down, complete the phrase by saying, 'As I have loved you.' Let these words speak directly to you. Know that you have been loved since you were formed in your mother's womb and that you will always be loved.

Memories and images of being loved and loving will come to mind. Be aware of them and receive them without being bound merely to the realm of thought. Above all else be open to sensing the presence of Love. God's love cannot be understood. It can however be experienced. Allow yourself to move deeper than thought to being renewed in an experience of the love that is everlasting.

After fifteen minutes of meditation begin to express your heart's desire to God in prayer. Our deepest desire is for love in its trueness, covered over as this may often be by false or confused desires. Give voice to the longing that is truest in you. Express it both for yourself and for the world. Finish by saying the Lord's Prayer.

6 ❖ Old Age and Wisdom

And the Holy Spirit rested on him
(Luke 2.25)

We have all seen a young child being held in the arms
of an old man or woman. Have we not felt at such
moments that the connection between the very old
and the very young can be profounder than that
between any other two stages in life? In part it is
because their closeness to birth at the one end of the
spectrum, and to death at the other, provides them
with a type of common ground. 'Naked I came from
my mother's womb, and naked shall I return there,' as
Job says.[1] Images of life beginning and life ending
merge in the meeting of the young and the old. But an
even deeper sense of connection is painted by St Luke
in his account of the presentation of the Christ-child
in the Jerusalem temple. Simeon, a devout old man on
whom 'the Holy Spirit rested', says Luke, is the one
who recognizes the light that is in the child. He takes
him in his arms and praises God. Similarly Anna, 'of
great age', described by Luke as praying in the temple
'night and day', perceives more deeply than what outward eye can see the hope that has been born with this
child. It is no coincidence that an old man and woman

of prayer are the ones to see these things. In their old age they have been given the grace of wisdom, and, as in St Matthew's account of the magi being guided to the Christ-child,[2] it is the wise who see what others do not.

What do we mean by the grace of wisdom? In part it is a way of seeing or understanding that grows out of experience. The wisdom tradition of the Old Testament saw this grace as having been 'poured out upon all the living',[3] but as coming to particular expression in those with an understanding that has been enriched by experience. The wise, says Solomon, 'know the things of old and infer the things to come'.[4] This is not to say that all those with experience are wise. We know old men and women who in their narrowness or bitterness have closed themselves off to the grace of wisdom. Scowling at life and suspicious they become like snappy disgruntled curs. Nor is it to say that wisdom emerges only in the old, for we see signs of it in people at almost every stage of life. Apart from old age, perhaps it is especially in the very young that we see marks of wisdom. These may be expressions of what St Paul called the 'foolishness' of wisdom,[5] but most of us will remember little children who have pointed far more profoundly to life's mysteries than our attempts at profundity later on. There was the little boy for instance who asked his older sister where God was. 'In our hearts,' she said, to which the boy sat looking slightly bemused before responding, 'So, God goes beat, beat, beat.' God, the very heartbeat of life. Is there a profounder comment on the mystery in which we live than that?

According to the wisdom tradition, wisdom was born with us in the womb.[6] How frustrating it therefore seems that having been so endowed at birth, and

71

reflecting aspects of wisdom in our early years, we then have to wait ninety-five years to recover it again! The truth of the gospel of course is that we do not have to wait that long. It is planted deep within, created as we are in the image of the One who is Wisdom. The grace of wisdom stirs within us at the different stages of life. It is like a sleeping beauty ever waiting to be further awakened. How then is this grace to be rediscovered and given expression in our lives? And what is it exactly about certain old men and women that releases this grace into the flowering of a wise spirit?

The Holy Spirit, says St Luke, 'rested' on Simeon. Although the Spirit is traditionally portrayed as active, rushing like wind and water or flaming forth like fire, the word here used is 'rested'. It suggests the easing up again or restfulness that can occur in the old. We some-times see in them a return of playfulness or a greater willingness to laugh again, both at themselves and at the silly things of life. 'Whoever loves wisdom loves life,' says Ecclesiasticus.[7] Some of this sheer delighting in life will not have been given much room since childhood, but the letting go of busy responsibilities and the sense of self-importance that can characterize the middle years releases the old simply to *be* again rather than feeling that they must always be *doing*. In 'A Song for Simeon', T. S. Eliot expresses the sense of sitting lightly to life that characterizes a wise old person:

> My life is light, waiting for the death wind,
> Like a feather on the back of my hand.[8]

We will all have memories of old men and women snoozing during the day, images of the letting go that is happening. One of the most colourful in my recollection is a recurring feature of St Andrew's Day celebrations in Edinburgh. The old Scottish Knights of the Thistle, clad in their rich green velvet cloaks, process with dignity to seats in the crossing of the cathedral, only to promptly fall into a deep sleep for the sermon. Those who have been busy during their earlier years are granted the right to doze in the evening of their lives.

The letting go that characterizes these final years is something that needs to happen in different ways at the different stages of life. Only thus will certain aspects of who we are be released. At the outward level there needs to be a letting go, or a restfulness, in order to make room for new ways of seeing and for deep creativities to emerge. It is a dying at one level to allow a fuller living at another. Sometimes it is when we are most relaxed that a new realization will surface into our consciousness. Often it will be a perspective on our lives or work that would not have emerged if we had remained only actively engaged. This dying to the outer in order to release something from within characterizes the great traditions of prayer and meditation. It is a becoming still outwardly so as to be more attentive to the inner reality of spirit.

When I once asked an old monk at Quarr Abbey what he did, he smiled in response and said, 'Nothing.' The same monk described himself in his old age as coming to believe more and more about less and less. The reality of course was that he was continuing to do and believe much, but the value of what he did and believed was rooted not in any outward status or claim but in the simple practice of being still. It was his commitment to being empty before God that gave him his inner certainty of strength and security. This letting go of the outward that is a mark of the old and wise is one that can release them from narrow prejudice and religious preconception. They are set free to see and respond in unbounded and unexpected ways. It was this in part that allowed Simeon and Anna to recognize the light of the Christ-child. Their perspective was deeper and broader than the traditional expectation that assumed the coming of God to be clothed in power and outward glory. Simeon had been longing for the restoration of Israel. It was the grace of wisdom that enabled him to see salvation as having come in this unexpected and unknown child.

Doing nothing of course is not necessarily of value in and by itself, for there is such a thing as wasting time fruitlessly. We can be very busy doing nothing. But, in St Luke's Gospel, Simeon and Anna are old people who in 'doing nothing' are looking and seeing more deeply. Anna as a widow has been released from certain outward responsibility and instead spends her time night and day in the temple. As Eliot says, it is a matter of putting off outward preoccupation and sense in order to see the 'intersection of the timeless with time'.[9] Such was the presentation of the Christ-child in the temple, and Anna saw it. Unpreoccupied with the outward she was alert to glimpsing the presence of the invisible in the midst of the visible. Like the intermingling of spirit and matter that is depicted in Celtic art's patterns of inseparably overlapping strands, so Anna perceived in the events of a particular moment an eternal presence.

There are men and women who on letting go of busy loads begin to be aware of dimensions of life that they may not have noticed or been committed to before. An old Scots Presbyterian woman in her nineties took up the daily practice of visiting St Giles' Cathedral to be still and to light a candle as a sign of her prayer.

Many Presbyterians will not even have seen a candle in church let alone take up the practice of lighting one every day, but such is the largeness of spirit in the wise to overcome the limitations of tradition. When she was asked one day by a visitor if, in this world of so much wrong and confusion, she could believe that there was a God, the old woman replied, 'I do not *believe* there is a God. I *know* there is a God.' In a sense only an old woman who prays daily has the right to speak with such certainty. In another sense of course she, in her daily practice of silence, is a sign of what all of us are needing to recover in our different ways if we are to regain wisdom's way of seeing.

The early Church encouraged the old, and particularly widows, to take on a greater inner responsibility as their outer responsibilities were lightened. A widow was viewed as able to make a commitment to prayer, not simply for herself but on behalf of the Church and even for the sake of the world. This was a great vocation that could come late in life. Something of this has been preserved over the centuries in the Church's contemplative orders, men and women praying on behalf of the Church and world. What has been lost however is a sense of all of us being called to a vocation of prayer, to be pursued in different ways at the different stages of our lives. A young mother's pattern of prayer will necessarily be very different from an old woman's. The time available, as well as the space, will likely be entirely different. The question we need to ask ourselves at every stage is, where are the side chapels of our lives? What are the times and places when we can enter silence even for a few minutes? It may be at a window or a quiet corner in our house. Similarly it may be in the garden or park or even on a train.

Whatever our schedule and responsibilities we need to be finding times and places to enter what Eliot called 'the still point of the turning world'.[10] That is the place from which all life has come, and in which we will be restored to our true selves. The busyness and action of our lives, he says:

> Brings knowledge of motion, but not of stillness;
> Knowledge of speech, but not of silence;
> Knowledge of words, and ignorance of the Word.[11]

To return again and again to the 'still point' is to orientate ourselves to what is most real and to be set free from limited confinements to the outward.

It is not particularly surprising that our Western world, characterized by a busy materialism, should also be a world that in many places has ceased to venerate old age. What is surprising is the extent to which we pretend that we will be forever young. As Ecclesiasticus wisely remarks, 'Do not disdain one who is old, for some of us are also growing old.'[12] If primary value however is attached to the outward, and to what one possesses and looks like and does, what will be the place given to the old? The way in which they are pushed to the edge of what is seen as important in our communities and families is a sign also of the rejection of what they represent. Old age is repeatedly devalued into an inferior state of being, regarded as a decline or fall from the fullness of life. We have forgotten the fruit that an old tree can bear, yielding an abundance that will far outweigh the crops of the young.

The early Celtic Christian teacher, Pelagius, in a letter to an elderly friend, reflected on the distinction between what the old and the young have to offer:

> We should distinguish between active love and
> passive love. Active love does good through outward
> and visible movement; passive love does good
> through inward and invisible movement. The
> young person serves others with his mind and his
> body; the old person serves others with his soul.[13]

Pelagius is pointing to the contribution of the wise as
something that is deeper than action and even than
thought. The story of the old man who had lost his
powers of speech and movement but who nevertheless
had a profound effect on those around him illustrates
this point. In a residential home where there were
plenty of others with outward faculties still intact, it
was around the paralysed old man that people would
gather. He communicated in his spirit a well-being and
peace that was deeper than utterance. It is something of
this that has been preserved in the Indian tradition of
the sanyassi, in which an old man late in life abandons
all outward claim to possessions and family status and
simply wanders as a holy man of prayer. In the East
such a man is marked not by what he does, nor even
necessarily by what he says or teaches, but by his spirit.
Similarly people will gather round a guru simply to
be in his presence, and in a sense to catch peace from
him at a level profounder than words. To recover a
reverence for wisdom as something that is deeper than
thought and action is a great challenge to our Western
world. No less significant is the recovery of the practice of being still as a way of becoming attentive to
the seeds of wisdom that have been planted in our own
depths.

Wise men and women see beneath the busyness of our
age and more deeply than the idolizing of appearances

and possessions. They see these things as vanishing like a shadow or, as Solomon says, 'like a ship that sails through the billowy water, and when it has passed no trace can be found, no track of its keel in the waves'.[14] There is in them no need to hide from who they are, from their age and wrinkling, for they know that they bear a beauty deeper than cosmetics and matured by many seasons of life. We will all have memories of the faces of old men and women that shine like hardened chestnuts. They are not ashamed to be themselves, says Ecclesiasticus,[15] nor are they hesitant to speak against wrong when it is right to rebuke and be silent when they have nothing to say.[16] There is no need to cover up the mistakes of their lives from which they have grown and become stronger within. There is no need to insist on simplistic answers and immediate solutions for they know the mystery of time's fullness and have acquired the endurance that comes with waiting.

Is not this the greatness of a Nelson Mandela today, the wisdom shaped by years of endurance? Such wisdom in the old is like a great tree that has stood the test of time. It may bear, both within itself as well as outwardly, the scars of struggle and of storms endured, but its mighty branches are like arms that have been strength- ened by roots that reach deep into the earth. Great trees become places of sanctuary and renewal. The leaves of such a tree, as St John the Divine sees, are for the healing of the nations.[17] Healing will come among us in our societies and world not simply by busy out- ward action but through work that is sustained by wisdom's depth of seeing and believing. 'The multitude of the wise', says Solomon, 'is the salvation of the world.'[18]

Probably one of the greatest examples in the twentieth century of integrating inner restfulness and outer action was the American Trappist monk Thomas Merton. His contribution to the peace movement was to insist that it was only by giving attention to the inner, and to the way of prayer and non-violence of heart, that we could arrive at a sense of measure in relation to outward action. He saw that the roots of justice and peace needed to be spiritual if they are to be sustained and integrated into the whole of life. In the tension between action and contemplation that all of us live in the midst of, it is an awareness of the inner that will undergird and strengthen us in the transformation of our lives together. The wise old person, in his shift of focus from outer reality towards inner reality, lives among us not as a sign of disparaging the outward and the physical but as a reminder that it is the spiritual that is at the heart of reality.

To say that wise men and women are like beautiful old trees deeply rooted is also to say that their wisdom did not grow in a day and a night. They have become what they are through years and years of openness to the springs of God's wisdom within them. Their wise spirit in old age is a valuation of what they have been over many seasons. In the midst of busyness at the different stages of life they have found time also to nurture the inner grace of wisdom. 'I preferred her to sceptres and thrones, and I accounted wealth as nothing in comparison with her,' says Solomon. 'Therefore I prayed, and understanding was given me; I called on God, and the spirit of wisdom came to me.'[19]

Exercise

In this Gospel story, when Simeon takes the Christ-child in his arms he blesses God and says, 'My eyes have seen your salvation' (Luke 2.30). It is the grace of wisdom that enables him to see salvation in the little child. Simeon's words can guide us in meditating on the grace of wisdom, given for us all.

Find a comfortable but alert position in which to sit and begin to repeat the prayer, 'My eyes have seen your salvation.' Sometimes it can be helpful to start a meditation by uttering the words aloud: 'My eyes have seen your salvation.' Gradually however begin to speak them silently within. You are speaking not to One who is distant from you, but to the One who is closer than your very breath.

Discover a rhythm for repeating the words that keeps time with your breathing. This can help to sustain a focus of inner attention. Try repeating the words as you breathe down. 'My eyes have seen your salvation.' The place of your salvation is deep within you, where God dwells. Then, as you breathe upwards, be aware of the restoration and wisdom that can issue up from that place into the whole of your life.

After fifteen minutes of prayerfully repeating these words, begin to express to God your heart's desires. What is it you are most deeply looking for in your life and for the world? Express this simply in prayer. Finish by saying the Lord's Prayer.

7 ❖ Death As Return

'Father, into your hands I commend my spirit'
(Luke 23.46)

How do we view the journey that awaits us all, and not only us but all that has been created? 'All that is of earth', says Ecclesiasticus, 'returns to earth, and what is from above returns above.'[1] The Celtic tradition of prayer in the Western Isles has two striking images for that journey. One is of death being like 'a river hard to see'. The phrase speaks in part of the unknowable dimension of death. We do not know precisely what death's waters are going to be like for us. We do not know when we shall enter them and what exactly is waiting for us on the other side. There is in us a fear, in many cases not so much about death itself as about dying, and the pain and grieving that accompany it. Jesus' reciting of the ancient words of faith from a psalm that is traditionally used at compline, 'Into your hands I commend my spirit',[2] do not detract from the agony that he experiences in facing death. 'Remove this cup from me,' he prays in the Garden of Gethsemane, as in anguish his sweat becomes like drops of blood falling to the ground.[3]

This combination of knowing where to look for

strength and yet at the same time not denying the sense of terror that is felt in the face of death is reflected in one of the Celtic prayers for protection:

> O Master endeared, . . .
> O Master beloved, . . .
> I beseech Thee with earnestness, . . .
> I beseech Thee with tearfulness, . . .
> That Thou not forsake me
> In the passion of my death.[4]

There is an understanding that our death and all death is to be interpreted in the light of Christ's passion. The Son of Man reveals in his suffering something of what is true for all people in their journey through death.

The second image from the Celtic tradition is that of being met on the other side of death's waters by the saints of heaven:

> Be each saint in heaven,
> Each sainted woman in heaven,
> Each angel in heaven
> Stretching their arms for you,
> Smoothing the way for you,
> When you go thither
> Over the river hard to see;
> Oh when you go thither home
> Over the river hard to see.[5]

The imagery is similar to that of being commended into the hands of God, being entrusted into the arms of those who have gone before. As Ecclesiasticus writes, 'Do not fear death's decree for you; remember those who have gone before you and those who will come after.'[6]

The combination of passing through waters and into

the arms of heaven's waiting women, speaks also of a type of birth journey. The sainted women are like the mid-wives of the life that we are born into through the contractions of death. Many who have experienced the loss of son or daughter, or husband or wife, have known their loved one's passage into death as being at a deeper level a birth journey. Death is like a womb that opens into the other dimension, expansive and unbounded. While it is strange and frightening it is also, as the Irish Carmelite priest Noel O'Donoghue says, the journey towards a 'freshness of dawn'.

If all that is seen, as the writer to the Hebrews says, has come forth from what cannot be seen, then death is the return of all that is visible into the invisible realm of God. We may not remember being in our mother's womb. Similarly, says St Augustine in his *Confessions*, we may not remember coming from God, but from God we have been born and to God we return. All that has been created is on that pilgrimage of return. As T. S. Eliot writes:

> We shall not cease from exploration
> And the end of all our exploring
> Will be to arrive where we started
> And know the place for the first time.[7]

Death returns us to our place of origin, even though as Eliot says, we are 'not the same people who left that station' at the beginning of the journey.[8] Life is a pilgrimage that leads us further into consciousness, through both joy and suffering.

When we stand in a great gathering of men and women, including children and infants, it can be difficult to comprehend that there is for each one a specific journey ahead through death. As Solomon says, 'There is for all one entrance into life, and one way out.'[9] Death may seem a distant reality, one that touches the lives only of people out there, but it is given for each one of us. The angel of death in time visits each one. As the grace of birth is given to all, so is the grace of death.

Perhaps even more difficult is to stand under open skies or beside what seems like infinite stretches of sea or high immovable mountains and to know that all that we see has its coming as well as its going. There will be a time when even 'the old eternal rocks', as the hymn of St Patrick calls them, will be no more. All things pass through that invisibly narrow aperture of death that seems to crush into non-existence everything that enters it. Edwin Muir, in his poem 'Journey Back', saw that every field of life will in time be 'white with harvest'.[10] How do we learn to live in relationship to this harvesting of all things? In part, says Muir, it is creation itself that can guide us. Each evening sky, he says, bright and golden, speaks of the harvest of that day. Death is present in each day's ending. It is present in each moment's passing, and the grace that accompanies it is one that we either respond to or reject repeatedly. A spirituality that is alert to creation, as is the Celtic, sees in death not a movement away from life but a grace through which we may move closer to life's source. A song from the Western Isles, chanted at the deathbed of a loved one, saw the grace of death as leading us to the home of the seasons:

Thou goest home this night to thy home of winter,
To thy home of autumn, of spring, and of summer;
Thou goest home this night to thy perpetual home.
. . .

84

Sleep, O sleep in the love of all loves;
Sleep, O beloved, in the Lord of life,
Sleep, O beloved, in the God of life![11]

As St Francis also put it in his great song of creation, death is the grace that leads us home.[12]

How then do we view our own death or the death of those whom we love? In the midst of the sorrow and often incomprehension that we feel, or in the midst of the anger, have we also eyes for seeing in death a hidden grace? Dare we say that the grace of return is to be looked for even in the ugliest and most unjust of deaths? In the Gospel accounts of the Easter story, the stone of the tomb in which the crucified Christ is laid is described as having been rolled away. The heart of the Christian mystery is not an avoidance of suffering but rather a conviction that the place of death is not closed in on itself. Is it possible to so approach the mass graves of a Rwanda or a former Yugoslavia? It was only days after the Dunblane massacre in Scotland in 1996 that a child from Portsmouth, in looking at a crucifix, said, 'That is like the Dunblane children.' We believe that the grace of moving into a further union with God was given to Jesus in his horrific death. Can we affirm that to be deeply true for all people, whether they die peacefully or violently, suddenly or expectedly?

The tendency has often been to try to shield children from the dark side of the Christ story. The prophet Isaiah's perspective on the suffering servant, while it is at the heart of our tradition and of Good Friday liturgies throughout the whole Church, is often excluded from the young:

He was despised and rejected by others;
a man of suffering and acquainted with infirmity;

and as one from whom others hide their faces
he was despised, and we held him of no account.[13]

In the religious education of children we have tended instead to concentrate on images of the good Jesus, gentle and kind. Should we wonder then why later in life the Christian inheritance for so many seems to be lacking? When they begin to witness and experience injustice and sorrows for themselves, have they then the tools to look for grace in those painful situations? Or do they simply begin to doubt the half-truths that the Church has given them in its avoidance of the reality of suffering and death for each one of us?

A woman commented that when in meditation her heart had been awakened it had been to an awareness of pain. The inner knowledge that characterizes Christian spirituality is not only an awareness of the light that the darkness has not overcome, as St John says,[14] but of the suffering within us and within all creation. Children in their own way are much more capable of looking at suffering and death than we give them credit for. A mother spoke of her little son's relationship with a neighbour who was dying of cancer. When death finally came she thought it would be best for the boy not to attend the service in the house next door, but he persisted in asking until she agreed. At the funeral his mother held him up so that he could look at the corpse laid out on the table. He gazed calmly at the body and then appeared to want to lean over to touch it, but in fact he was getting down to cross the room in order to give the widow a hug. In a child there can be an awareness and sensitivity that are deeper than conscious understanding.

Those who have grown up in cultures that continue the wake tradition are familiar with the practice of watching and grieving by the dead before burial and then merry-making afterwards. They speak matter-of-factly about seeing bodies laid out on family tables and peeking through the doorways of houses to see who is on the table and what they look like. Children can learn to see death as part of what we are given in life. Is the reality not that, rather than protecting our children from confronting death, we are often simply trying to protect ourselves? It is a reflection of the denial of death that so pervades our Western culture. The attempt to push the dying and the dead to the periphery of daily life, to the extent that very few of us have any natural point of contact with the dying or with the bodies of those who have died, almost creates the impression that we are not all going to die. The Scriptures state clearly that 'the human body is a fleeting thing'.[15] Death is not the end, but rather a doorway through which we pass. As Eliot writes:

> We must be still and still moving
> Into another intensity
> For a further union, a deeper communion
> Through the dark cold and the empty desolation,
> The wave cry, the wind cry, the vast waters
> Of the petrel and the porpoise. In my end is my
>   beginning.[16]

To acknowledge death as part of the pilgrimage that we are given is to be better prepared to look also for the grace that God desires to give us in dying. It is the grace of moving further into life.

The priest in Shakespeare's *Twelfth Night* measures time in terms of death. Recounting a nuptial that he has just presided over, he says:

87

Since when, my watch hath told me, toward my
   grave
I have travelled but two hours.[17]

This is not a morose perspective but rather part of
knowing himself, and therefore knowing that all things
are moving towards death. To name the reality of death
for ourselves, and to believe that in it is a grace that can
be responded to, is to be liberated, whether we live or
whether we die. A wise old lady said to a younger
woman who felt that it was morbid to have a discussion about death, 'You do not have to keep talking
about it, but at one point or another you have to look
it in the face if you are to be freed from it.'

Jesus' words of commending his spirit into the hands
of God are not simply his death prayer but the prayer
of his life. His life had been a letting go to God, a
dying, as he said, in order to live. 'Father, into your
hands I commend my spirit' can be the prayer by which
we open ourselves to the grace of dying in every
moment of life. This is not just something that we will
either receive or reject at some stage in the future
when we are approaching the end of our journey. 'The
time of death', as Eliot wrote, 'is every moment.'[18] The
graces of dying and rising are present for us in every
experience of life, from the smallest of things to the
greatest. To respond will affect the way we let go of
each day as well as the way in which we let go of our
lives.

Many of us will have witnessed the transformation
of spirit in people about to die who have let go. Faces
that had been marked with tension or bitterness can be
changed into calm and even radiant looks. A woman
spoke of her sister as having died after a long struggle

with cancer. The countenance that had been racked with pain for weeks became instead at the hour of her death that of a youthful woman. The prayers in the Celtic tradition sometimes refer to death as 'the great sleep of Jesus'. It is described as 'the young sleep' and 'the restoring sleep' as well as 'the sleep of Jesus' wound' and 'the sleep of Jesus' grief'.[19] In each moment of death a grace of new life is being offered. This is not to detract from the pain of loss or the grieving that accompanies it, but to point to the grace within death, shrouded as it may well be in darkness.

To commend ourselves into the hands of God is not to hand ourselves over to One who is distant from us. 'Underneath', say the Scriptures 'are the everlasting arms.'[20] It is to pass through the net of death rather than being forever ensnared in it. It is to allow ourselves to fall deeper than dying into what is deepest and truest within us. It is a returning to the heart of our lives and of all life. As the old Celtic prayer says:

> As Thou wast before
> At my life's beginning,
> Be Thou so again
> At my journey's end.[21]

In both our living and our dying it is a being renewed in that part of ourselves that is rooted in Eden.

Exercise

Find a comfortable but alert position in which to sit. Be aware of your body and your breathing, but also of what is around you. Meditation is not about closing yourself off to the outward but about moving more deeply into awareness, of both the inner and the outer.

Begin to repeat silently the words of Jesus, 'Father, into your hands I commend my spirit.' It may be that the phrase needs to be abbreviated. Simplify it so that it becomes yours. Let it express your deepest reality.

Allow the repetition of the words to find a natural rhythm in keeping with your breathing. 'Into your hands I commend my spirit.' Repeat the words as you breathe down. Be assured that you are offering yourself not to One who is far off but to the One who is near. God is at the heart of your true self. These words of commitment are to what is deepest and truest within you. Then as you breathe upwards be aware of drawing from those true depths. Sense that you are being renewed by the Life within you that is deeper even than death.

After fifteen minutes of silent meditation on these words begin to express your heart's desires for yourself and your world. Know that in so doing you join your voice to Christ's ongoing prayer for the life of the world. Finish with the Lord's Prayer.

Appendix:
A Guide for Group Use

Introduction

Review with the group the main theme of the book's relevant chapter. Make it clear however that the focus of the meeting is not the material that has been read but rather the group meditation that is to follow. The written material is simply a preparation for the latter.

Indicate the overall shape of the meeting, with a reminder that the method of Scripture meditation to be used is *lectio divina*, consisting of *lectio* (reading), *meditatio* (meditation), and *oratio* (prayer).

Preparation

Encourage people to find a comfortable but alert position for the meditation.

Begin by saying together the prayer for purity:

> *Almighty God,*
> *to whom all hearts are open,*
> *all desires known,*
> *and from whom no secrets are hidden:*
> *cleanse the thoughts of our hearts*

by the inspiration of your Holy Spirit,
that we may perfectly love you,
and worthily magnify your holy name;
through Christ our Lord.
Amen.

Lectio

Remind the group of the Scripture phrase to be used for meditation.

Read aloud the words of the exercise at the end of the relevant chapter (with the exception of the exercise's last paragraph).

Meditatio

Repeat again the words to be used for meditation.
Allow a full fifteen minutes for silence.

Oratio

Adapting the words of the last paragraph of the exercise, lead the group from meditation into silent prayer.
Ensure a full five minutes for prayer.
Finish with the Lord's prayer:

Our Father in heaven,
hallowed be your name,
your kingdom come,
your will be done
on earth as in heaven.
Give us today our daily bread.
Forgive us our sins
as we forgive those who sin against us.

Lead us not into temptation
but deliver us from evil.
For the kingdom, the power,
and the glory are yours
now and for ever.
Amen.

Small Group Conversation

Encourage people to form groups of two or three to talk about the experience of the meditation, and any of the memories or images that may have arisen.

Allow at least ten minutes for this.

Large Group Discussion

Call people back into the full group and invite them to share anything they may wish to from their individual meditations or small group conversations. Allow these contributions now to form the basis of group discussion on the theme of the meditation.

Allow at least thirty minutes for this time of shared reflection.

Close the meeting by saying together:

The grace of our Lord Jesus Christ,
the love of God,
and the fellowship of the Holy Spirit,
be with us all evermore.
Amen.

Notes

Introduction

1. Edwin Muir, 'One Foot in Eden', *Selected Poems*, Faber and Faber, 1965, p. 80.
2. J. Philip Newell, *Listening for the Heartbeat of God: a Celtic spirituality*, SPCK, 1997.
3. Muir, 'One Foot in Eden', p. 80.
4. Matthew 13.44.
5. T. S. Eliot, 'East Coker – Four Quartets', *Collected Poems (1909–62)*, Faber and Faber, 1963, p. 203.
6. Eliot, 'The Dry Salvages – Four Quartets', p. 213.
7. John 1.9.
8. John Cassian, *Conferences*, Paulist Press, 1985, 10.14.
9. Cassian, 10.10.
10. Cassian, 10.14.
11. Cassian, 10.11.
12. Cassian, 10.11.
13. Psalm 46.10.
14. Cassian, 10.13.
15. Clifton Wolters, tr., *The Cloud Of Unknowing*, Penguin Books, 1961, Chapter 7.
16. Psalm 70.1.
17. Cassian, 10.11.

Chapter 1: Birth and Holiness

1. John 1.9.

2. Hebrews 11.3.
3. Robert Van de Weyer (ed.), *The Letters of Pelagius*, Arthur James Ltd, 1995, 36.
4. Job 38.8.
5. Job 12.10.
6. Genesis 1.31.
7. John 1.3.
8. R. S. Thomas, 'A. D.', *Counterpoint*, Bloodaxe Books, 1990, p. 42.
9. W. B. Yeats, 'The Two Trees', *Selected Poetry*, Macmillan, 1971, p. 20.
10. William Wordsworth, 'Ode: Intimations of Immortality from Recollections of Early Childhood', V 1.62–65.
11. Anthony de Mello, *Wellsprings*, Doubleday, 1986, p. 219.
12. Romans 8.22f.

Chapter 2: Childhood and Innocence

1. William Blake, 'A Cradle Song', *A Selection of Poems and Letters*, Penguin, 1977, p. 33.
2. Blake, 'The Little Girl Lost', p. 44.
3. Blake, 'The Little Girl Found', p. 46.
4. Wordsworth, 'Intimations of Immortality', I 1.1–5.
5. Edwin Muir, *An Autobiography*, Hogarth Press, 1980, p. 18.
6. Muir, 'The Original Place', *Selected Poems*, p. 31.
7. Muir, 'One Foot in Eden', *Selected Poems*, p. 81.

Chapter 3: Adolescence and Awakening

1. Jeremiah 33.3.
2. From S. T. Coleridge's 'Notebooks', as quoted by C. G. Jung, *Memories, Dreams, Reflections*, Collins, 1964, p. 9.
3. Saint Augustine, *Confessions*, translated by R. S. Pine-Coffin, Penguin Books, 1961, Book X, chapter 27.
4. Matthew 9.1–8.
5. John Scotus Eriugena, 'Homily on the Prologue to the Gospel of St John', *The Voice of the Eagle*, Lindisfarne Press, 1990, p. 49.
6. John 1.1, 3.

7. John 1.5.
8. Revelation 9.1f.
9. Julian of Norwich, *Revelations of Divine Love*, translated by Clifton Wolters, Penguin Books, 1966, chapter 67.
10. Luke 15.11–32.
11. Julian of Norwich, *In Love Enclosed*, translated by Sheila Upjohn, Darton, Longman and Todd, 1985, chapter 32.

Chapter 4: Early Adulthood and Passion

1. Matthew 15.32.
2. Luke 7.13.
3. Luke 19.42.
4. Isaiah 56.7.
5. Jeremiah 31.3.
6. Hosea 11.8.
7. H. A. Williams, *Some Day I'll Find You*, Fount, 1984.
8. 1 Corinthians 3.16.
9. Matthew 6.6.
10. Psalm 46.10.
11. K. White, *The Bird Path*, Mainstream, 1989, p. 146.
12. Matthew 5.8.
13. Blake, 'A Memorable Fancy', p. 101.
14. Revelation 3.16.
15. 'The Rule of St Columba' as quoted by Ian Finlay, *Columba*, Gollancz, 1979, p. 176.
16. Amos 5.21, 24.
17. George Herbert, 'Love'.
18. Luke 23.28.
19. John 11.35.
20. Luke 19.41.
21. Galatians 5.23.
22. Luke 9.23.
23. Luke 9.24.

Chapter 5: Middle Years and Commitment

1. Augustine, *Confessions*, Book X, chapter 10.
2. D. Bohm, *Wholeness and the Implicate Order*, Ark, 1990.

3. Muir, 'The Journey Back', p. 60.
4. Colossians 1.16.
5. Romans 8.2.
6. Matthew 22.39.
7. Revelation 2.4–5.
8. Psalm 27.10.
9. Saint Teresa, 'The Seventh Mansions', *The Interior Castle*, translated by the Benedictines of Stanbrook, London, 1921.
10. Matthew 5.45.
11. Luke 23.34.
12. John 10.30.

Chapter 6: Old Age and Wisdom

1. Job 1.21.
2. Matthew 2.1f.
3. Ecclesiasticus 1.10.
4. Wisdom 8.8.
5. 1 Corinthians 1.25.
6. Ecclesiasticus 1.14.
7. Ecclesiasticus 4.12.
8. Eliot, 'A Song for Simeon', p. 111.
9. Eliot, 'The Dry Salvages – Four Quartets', p. 212.
10. Eliot, 'Burnt Norton – Four Quartets', p. 191.
11. Eliot, 'The Eagle Soars in the Summit of Heaven – The Rock', p. 161.
12. Ecclesiasticus 8.6.
13. *The Letters of Pelagius*, 74.
14. Wisdom 5.10.
15. Ecclesiasticus 4.20.
16. Ecclesiasticus 20.1.
17. Revelation 22.2.
18. Wisdom 6.24.
19. Wisdom 7.7–8.

Chapter 7: Death As Return

1. Ecclesiasticus 40.11.
2. Psalm 31.5.

3. Luke 22.39f.
4. Alexander Carmichael (ed.), *Carmina Gadelica* III, Scottish Academic Press, 1976, p. 81.
5. *Carmina Gadelica* III, p. 203.
6. Ecclesiasticus 41.3.
7. Eliot, 'Little Gidding – Four Quartets', p. 222.
8. Eliot, 'The Dry Salvages – Four Quartets', p. 210.
9. Wisdom 7.6.
10. Muir, 'The Journey Back', p. 66.
11. *Carmina Gadelica* III, p. 383.
12. Saint Francis, 'The Canticle of Brother Sun'.
13. Isaiah 53.3.
14. John 1.5.
15. Ecclesiasticus 41.11.
16. Eliot, 'East Coker – Four Quartets', pp. 203–4.
17. William Shakespeare, *Twelfth Night*, V, i, 160–61.
18. Eliot, 'The Dry Salvages – Four Quartets', p. 211.
19. *Carmina Gadelica* III, p. 383.
20. Deuteronomy 33.27.
21. *Carmina Gadelica* III, p. 65.